QUEENSLAND
EVERYTHING YOU EVER WANTED TO KNOW BUT WERE AFRAID TO ASK

MARK BAHNISCH is the founder of the award-winning political blog *Larvatus Prodeo* and his commentaries and analyses have been published in *The Monthly*, *Crikey*, *New Matilda*, *The Drum*, the *Australian Financial Review*, *Australian Literary Review* and elsewhere.

In early 2015, Mark wrote a series of analytical articles on the Queensland election for *Guardian Australia*. He covered the 2006 Queensland election for *Crikey*, and was a key writer for its 2009 campaign blog, *Pineapple Party Time*. In 2012, as the director of FAQ Research, he again partnered with *Crikey* to edit an issue investigating coal seam gas and the state election, called 'Behind the Seams'. He now blogs at *The New Social Democrat*.

Mark has a PhD in sociology from the Queensland University of Technology, and has lived in Brisbane for most of his life.

QUEENSLAND
EVERYTHING YOU EVER WANTED TO KNOW BUT WERE AFRAID TO ASK

MARK BAHNISCH

NEWSOUTH

A NewSouth book

Published by
NewSouth Publishing
University of New South Wales Press Ltd
University of New South Wales
Sydney NSW 2052
AUSTRALIA
newsouthpublishing.com

© Mark Bahnisch 2015
First published 2015

10 9 8 7 6 5 4 3 2 1

This book is copyright. Apart from any fair dealing for the purpose of private study, research, criticism or review, as permitted under the Copyright Act, no part of this book may be reproduced by any process without written permission. Inquiries should be addressed to the publisher.

National Library of Australia Cataloguing-in-Publication entry
Creator: Bahnisch, Mark, author.
Title: Queensland: Everything you ever wanted to know but were afraid to ask / Mark Bahnisch.
ISBN: 9781742234342 (paperback)
   9781742241999 (ePub/Kindle)
   9781742247281 (ePDF)
Notes: Includes index.
Subjects: Political parties – Queensland.
  Political campaigns – Queensland.
  Australians – Queensland – Attitudes.
  Queensland – Politics and government.
  Queensland – Social life and customs.
  Queensland – Social conditions.
  Queensland – Description and travel.
Dewey Number: 324.09943

Design Josephine Pajor-Markus
Cover design Natalie Winter
Printer Griffin Press

All reasonable efforts were taken to obtain permission to use copyright material reproduced in this book, but in some cases copyright could not be traced. The author welcomes information in this regard.

This book is printed on paper using fibre supplied from plantation or sustainably managed forests.

CONTENTS

We have never been modern   1

1 Tales from the Cold Ghost   9
2 Is Queensland different?   24
3 Written out of *Neighbours*   37
4 Good coffee comes to Brisbane   57
5 Reform from unexpected places   80
6 Enter Bob Katter, the ghost at the feast   103
7 Campbell goes early   127

This is Queensland, anything can happen   153

Notes on sources   165
Acknowledgments   167
Index   169

WE HAVE NEVER BEEN MODERN

In 1999, Rosie Scott wrote in *The Red Heart*:

> Queensland seems to have a similar meaning for Australian writers as the Deep South has for American writers, as a kind of rich seedbed for the original, the flamboyant, the decadent, the extreme. It is definitely partly to do with the landscape. In Brisbane, for instance, the rickety old wooden Queenslanders drenched in bougainvillea, the palms, the astounding number of birds even in Red Hill where I lived, the jacarandas, all are unique in Australia … There is a sense of limitless space … It is also something to do with the extremes you find in Queensland too – the turbulence of the politics and the tendency to

> authoritarian government whatever the party, the corruption and ruthlessness on one hand, the idealism on the other ... There are possibilities in Queensland – eccentricities, ambiguities, extremes – that are particularly evocative for writers who are born or live here for awhile.

Such quotes are multiple, and return again and again to the same motifs, suggesting a commonality of experience but also an inability to quite pin down the state of Queensland. It's spacious, but it can feel intimate. It's authoritarian, but there's a sense of freedom because you can disappear and reappear and reinvent yourself. It's cruel, but its dreams are big ones. Extremes are normal in Queensland.

Premier Campbell Newman, soon to be a byword for extremism, abolished the Queensland Premier's Literary Awards as one of his first acts after his lopsided landslide victory in 2012. Novelist and screenwriter Gerard Lee wryly observed in 2002 that French theory had never really resonated in Queensland, a state where it was so hard to be a writer that no one was particularly happy about contemplating 'the death of the author', since poverty and lack of recognition seemed like it was threatening precisely that fate for individual authors. Writers have often beaten a path out of the state, or like Xavier Herbert, come here to rest in unlikely nooks. Newman was defeated after only one term and his successor, Annastacia Palaszczuk, struck a contrasting note by naming herself Minister for the Arts on assuming office, portending a swing of the pendulum for writers and artists.

This book is all about the constant tension exemplified in Queensland's distinctive political culture and history between the old and the new, between the extremes. This state, I shall argue, is always caught in that moment, at once facing a bright and modern future and teetering on the brink of a darker and murkier past. When Newman was elected, it was booted about that a coal seam gas well had been drilled on the Bjelke-Petersen family property at Bethany, just outside Kingaroy. It was said that Joh's grave had been disturbed, and his spirit now wandered powerfully over the land again. This probably isn't true, but Queensland is full of tales like this, and they often speak a truth.

It might seem odd to frame a book on Queensland by quoting French sociologist Bruno Latour's *We Have Never Been Modern* title but, then, Gerard Lee, on his first visit to Europe, found himself in Paris writing a novel about … Brisbane. And the author of this particular book is a sociologist. Also, notorious former premier, Sir Johannes Bjelke-Petersen, thought of himself as modern, always keen to see cranes on the skyline, not happy if Queensland wasn't surpassing everywhere else in generating wealth from its soil. What is modernity, though?

The Latin word *modernus* derived from *modo*, meaning 'just now', doesn't signify what we think modern means. It's much more clearly temporal, having the sense of something that has just happened, just now, only an instant ago. It captures that fleeting sense of the present, its inability to be grasped. The Romans, if they had the concept we have of modern, would not have approved. For Romans, anything that was a departure from *mos maiorum*, 'the way of our ancestors', was terrible, and would probably require expiation. The new was not good, the old celebrated.

It wasn't really until the Renaissance that modern came to have the meaning we now ascribe to it, and then it was a contrast with the ancient, the classical, the Roman and the Greek, which was absolutely better than the new. It was necessary to ensure that the new conformed to the ancient, and that's why, in a nutshell, St Peter's in Rome doesn't look that dissimilar to that incredible first-century edifice on the other side of the Tiber, the Pantheon. It was only with the Enlightenment that the *Querelle des Anciens et des Modernes* ('the quarrel of the ancients and the moderns') could launch itself, a wrangle between the forces of rationality and those of immemorial custom. Something new was possible under the sun, it was asserted, and that something could be good.

It's a long, long story, but it's also the origin of our transvaluation of modernity, our valuation of modernity as shiny, new and good, our myth of progress and our obsession with forward movement and change. Latour's point, in what is really an anthropology of science and technology, is that modernity is founded on a distinction between nature and culture that we can no longer maintain, that anti-modernity and post-modernity are just reflections of the fundamental inability of modernity to separate out these two domains.

My point is somewhat different, much less sociological, although hopefully complementary. Maybe it's a little more influenced by those political economists and historians who teach us that things we think have been superseded – for instance, exchange by barter – never really go away and continue to play a role in the most hypermodern economies. I would suggest, quite simply, that the new is always in tension with the old, that we never escape the legacy of the old, and that the path to modernity is strewn with obstacles.

I think Queensland's story exemplifies this argument. Queensland has often been seen both as a provincial land of reactionary conservatism and as an exemplar of development at all costs. At the same time, the state was a laboratory for radical movements when it was still a colony, sending forth William Lane and his colonists to Paraguay, and giving birth to the Labour (now Labor) Party. The Shearer's Strike of the 1890s had its epicentre in Queensland, and Queensland was the first state to see Labor govern for decades. Former Russian Prime Minister Alexander Kerensky, the one Vladimir Lenin overthrew, lived in Brisbane from 1945 to 1946, and I've met people who knew him. Queensland abolished capital punishment in 1922, and New South Wales not until 1984.

Whether it's been perceived as a tabula rasa for utopianism or as the ultimate frontier of violent *terra nullius*, there's a shimmering quality to the state, a sense that it's not quite palpable, that anything can, and does, happen north of the Tweed. That could be something incredibly reactionary, something just crazy, or something incredibly radical. One thing you can say about the state's politics is that they're never, ever, boring. Big personalities abound, and following their thrills and spills can be a wild ride.

A debate in the 1970s and 1980s about Queensland's difference ignored a lot of its actual difference, and many on the left and of civil libertarian inclination worked long and hard for decades to assimilate the state to something akin to 'east coast normal', to flatten out its eccentricities, and to, well, modernise. These impulses, very strong ones, arguably stronger than the struggle of Joh Bjelke-Petersen to hold back the tide, and of some of his successors to turn back the clock, are quite understandable. But they often led to overreach, to a certain complacency, a desire to believe that the spectres of the dark forces of the past had been laid to rest.

It was impossible to believe this in the face of Campbell Newman's stunning electoral victory in 2012, and even less so as he governed. It was too easy to laugh at Bob Katter in 2012 when he launched his eponymous party's 'arts policy' on the Gold Coast, surrounded by young women in bikinis, and declared that he intended to take the state back to the 1980s (at least).

On the other hand, the huge swings back to Labor in this year's state election, not quite strong enough to deliver majority government but strong enough to ensure that Labor governs again under Premier Annastacia Palaszczuk, might give rise to a view that Queensland is topsy-turvy land, the site of wild swings of the electoral pendulum. And it can be, but it's also a state that had no change of government from 1932 to 1957 – really, that was only because of the Labor Split, which was a different phenomenon in the Sunshine State than in Victoria – and then again no change of government until 1989, when Wayne Goss defeated the shambolic remnants of the National Party regime. Big swings and lopsided victories do happen, but the meltdown of Tony Abbott's leadership that followed Campbell Newman's defeat in very quick succession indeed suggests that rather than Queensland continuing to be different from Australia, that Australia may be becoming more like Queensland. It's the task of this book to work through this claim.

So, is Queensland different? Yes, in the past. Will it be different into the future? In many, many ways that is a question that will be answered, at least provisionally, by what flows from this year's election, not just in Queensland but in the rest of the country. Whether or not the Labor Party can govern successfully will reveal how resilient 'new Queensland' is as against the 'old Queensland' of unfettered development, contempt for greenies and free speech and for the basics of liberal democracy. Campbell Newman appeared to represent an urban, if not urbane, style of governance, but that was exposed by his combative premiership as chimerical. So those outside the state should not be indifferent to Queensland's difference. Consider that the state has given the nation both Kevin Rudd and Dame Quentin Bryce, but also Pauline Hanson and Clive Palmer. What happens in Queensland matters.

1

TALES FROM THE COLD GHOST

> It's always been that way. Queensland was appallingly governed, right from the start. Go back a century – the big pastoralists owned the government then, and sheep were all they cared about. Meanwhile we were falling behind the southern states in everything else – industry, infrastructure, education. People were starting to wonder why. So the parliament said to the voters, it doesn't matter if you're poor. You're tougher than those southern states, you don't need good roads, or good schools, you're harder than that, you're different. Ignore anyone from the south who laughs at us, ignore anyone who suggests things could be better. In fact, be suspicious of anyone who says things could be better. They don't understand the Queensland way.
>
> – Andrew McGahan, *Last Drinks*, 2000

The 1993 federal election was supposedly unlosable for John Hewson, but was nevertheless won by Paul Keating. And it was won with a swag of seats in Queensland, which is always more important to national political outcomes than the fabled western Sydney, where most of the seats swing only when the Labor Party is in dire trouble. More of that later, suffice it to say now that federal politics in Queensland is much more fluid.

On 13 March that year, I was staffing a polling booth at the Coomera State School. Coomera is one of those pleasant districts that is either on the north of the Gold Coast or the south of Logan, depending on which way you're heading. Dreamworld was there even back in 1993, but the newly developed housing estates seemed an imposition on rolling farmland. The school itself, an old weatherboard country edifice, had a beautiful outlook up on a hill overlooking the Coomera River, with two straight lines of pine trees shading the drive. This had been Russ Hinze country under long-time Queensland Premier Joh Bjelke-Petersen. Hinze, the notorious 'Minister for Everything', had once advocated 'castration' and 'amputation' for sex offenders on ABC TV, and another time lamented the disappearance of canvas bench seats in cinemas because 'that was where [he had] learnt to make love'. Charged after the Fitzgerald Inquiry with multiple corruption offences, the larger-than-life character died of cancer before he could be brought to trial.

TALES FROM THE COLD GHOST

The National Party volunteers, old blokes with bowed legs and Akubras shading their gnarled faces, were from Hinze's era. The Liberal Party volunteer was a blow-in from Melbourne. It's hard to know why anyone of such a faith would have travelled so far north to exile himself from Jeff Kennett's neo-liberal utopia in the making. A neat blue baseball cap protected his face from the sun. Cameron Dick, later a minister in the Bligh Government and now the Health Minister in the new Palaszczuk Government, was with me at Coomera, flying the Labor flag earlier in the morning. But, as was the way, for most of the day in this still rural outpost I was alone in handing out for the ALP.

Sallyanne Atkinson, formerly a popular Brisbane Liberal Lord Mayor, was making her second (and as it turned out, last unsuccessful) run for federal parliament. A little bit of colour was provided by the intermittent presence of another woman, incongruously dressed in hippie garb, representing the Confederate Action Party, which was all about imminent invasions from Indonesia and UN 'world government' conspiracies, and tended to poll surprisingly well in the bits of Queensland where everyone owned a lot of guns. CAP later folded into One Nation, but Pauline Hanson was probably making fish and chips that day in 1993. I don't know. The day, though, was good humoured, breezy and unrushed with added jocularity provided by the fact our Victorian blow-in understood absolutely nothing about Queensland. I hate to confess it, but the rest of us enjoyed ourselves by having fun with his failure to get things. In the universal parlance of the country Queenslander, he wasn't 'from round here'.

About lunchtime, a uniformed senior sergeant of police strode up with a swagger, taking only the Nationals' how-to-vote card. The Liberal fellow, with a look of shock, said, 'I think I saw that guy vote at another booth this morning!' Perhaps all cops look the same in the bright light of the sun.

'Don't worry mate, he's okay, he's one of Russ' boys', said the Nat. 'Russ'll look after him.' The Liberal replied, reasonably enough, that the former Minister for Everything was dead.

'Naah, mate', drawled the Nat, alluding to kings who slumber beneath mountains ready to save their people in times of trial, 'he's just sleeping. Don't you worry about that, mate. Over there, in a cave in that hill.' Vote early and vote often was one hallmark of Joh Bjelke-Petersen's regime, and the dead voted too, in numbers, particularly in close by-elections.

The Nats of old could surprise with their erudition and their humour. They were kind to young Labor folks, too, maybe because I was able to claim some family connections more often than not. It wasn't my lot of German Lutherans, but a small white wooden Lutheran Church still stood at nearby Bethania, its miniature graveyard a testament to generations of German immigrant farmers, even if the redbrick suburbs had long supplanted the market gardens and farmlands in the Logan Valley.

In 1990, I'd had a similar mission to the one I pursued in 1993, but on election day that year I was standing at a much smaller country school, Greenmount, on the road between Warwick and Toowoomba, west of the Great Divide. Nestled between Cambooya and Allora, once known as Emu Creek, Greenmount is more village than town, and was where Arthur Hoey Davis, aka Steele Rudd of 'Dad and Dave' fame, had attended school. We had a visit from the local member, Labor's David Beddall, whose electorate kept getting stretched out of natural shape and extended from its heartland in solid Labor Inala every which way into the bush. Beddall, rightly, served his constituents just as respectfully in Warwick and the Lockyer Valley as in Logan, and so Labor could actually rely on up to 30 per cent of the vote in some of these small hamlets. I also won a few votes for Hawkie that day, explaining to old DLP voters that he was definitely anti-communist. That year, Sallyanne Atkinson had been represented only by a sign left by a Liberal in the morning. Liberalism, whatever it stood for under Andrew Peacock and later John Hewson, was conspicuous mainly in its absence.

When a Labor voter approached, the district's quota of old blokes in Akubras helpfully told me, 'He used to be a railway worker, he's one of yours'. I'll never forget an old fella driving up in an enormous 1950s Buick, beautifully maintained. He was one of the patriarchs of 'round here', a venerable grazier. At lunchtime, when I was hot and tired, one of the Nats offered to hand out my Labor how-to-votes while I walked 300 metres up the road to get lunch from the pub. I trusted him to do so. Perhaps one reason why the old blokes were always so friendly was that the real rivalry was between Nationals and Liberals outside Brisbane, and Labor and Nats more often than not shared common interests, and not just electorally, as the Country Party style of politics of the day was quite collectivist.

Another of my Coomera stories from that fateful day in 1993 was that my new friend, the old Nat, again had a lend of the Liberal bloke when a gust of wind had blown down the John Hewson sign from its perch on a tree above the school gate: 'Mate, the tide has just turned, it's not good for your bloke. Keating's won this thing.' This was one o'clock in the afternoon, or thereabouts, a little while after the senior sergeant had gone about his rounds, perhaps onto the next polling booth. Again, our Victorian blow-in didn't get it – there was no rationality in the claim. He babbled about polls and Fightback, and was finally reduced to saying, 'But how could you know?' The old bloke might have been having a lend of him, but, then, he was actually right. What this Victorian didn't get, in the final analysis, is that Queensland is not always rational; often it feels more like a realm of magic realism.

JASPER AND TIFFANY GO TO EAST GREENMOUNT

There was a story that used to do the rounds when I was younger, a variant on the urban (or in this case) rural myth about an unsuspecting city lad or laddette, naive to the folkways of the bush, who came to a nasty end in a country pub somewhere. Let's say the dude's name was Jasper, it's about 1987, and he and his girlfriend Tiffany have hopped into a racing-green MG and gone for a drive to Greenmount. Jasper's in new RM Williams boots and spotless moleskins, coupled with blue denim Country Road shirt. Tiffany's wearing a pastel pink Lacoste polo shirt with the collar turned up, nautical shorts and boat shoes. They park the MG and stride into the Wheatsheaf Hotel in East Greenmount, a beautiful weatherboard pub with iron verandahs with prominent yellow XXXX banners hung on them.

Saddling up to the bar, the bar bloke greets them: 'Dave.'

'No, no, my name is Jasper, and this is Tiffany.'

'All right, mate, I'm Dave. What'll youse have?'

'A Powers, thanks, mate', says Jasper, while Tiffany pipes up, 'a Fluffy Duck, please!' It's 1987, remember. Meanwhile, a few old blokes, possibly the same old blokes who hand out how-to-votes for the Nats, in identikit battered Akubras and work wear or soiled moleskins, start to mutter, 'I don't think they're from round here'. Dave, whose reflex is to pour a XXXX from the tap, interjects,

'I reckon they're from Brisbane'.

This might or might not be the country life Jasper and Tiffany have come to see, but they're getting thirsty.

'How about those drinks, Dave?' insists Jasper.

'Oh, sorry, mate, did you say two pots of XXXX?'

'No, we ordered a Powers and a Fluffy Duck, thank you very much.'

'No', drawls Dave, 'I coulda sworn you said two pots of XXXX'. There are more intense quizzical looks from the other end of the bar, and 'Definitely not from round here' can be heard, with 'Must be from Brisbane', echoing closely behind.

I like to think the story ends well, but you can probably figure out the alternative endings. Greenmount is a nice place, and the old fellows are inclined to be courtly, some of them the descendants of graziers who opened up the district, at the cost of the blackfellas let's not forget, back in the 1840s. I'm not saying Tara, further north on the Western Downs, isn't a nice place, but it's reputed that some folk there go armed in the streets, and the Commercial Hotel, a grand building that has definitely seen better days, doesn't present a welcoming aspect on first sight. Once you go in, it's hospitable and a welcome respite from the heat, but without too much imagination you could picture a pool cue meeting Jasper, if he'd gone there, in a way he hadn't quite envisioned. There are probably horror stories that start out like this but, as we know, they're mostly and no doubt unfairly set in Tasmania.

Anyway, long after the Jaspers and Tiffanies graduated (probably from the University of Queensland) and settled down to lucrative legal practices, I had a beer at Mary's Commercial Hotel in Dalby, described on its website as among the 'oldest and most legendary pubs on the Western Downs'. In case you're wondering why I seem to know so much about the pubs west of the range, it's partly because I have family connections 'round there', partly because I spent some time researching the impacts of coal seam gas on rural towns, and partly because I like the place. Also, it's hot on the Downs and beer is cold. I recall seeing at Mary's one of the now ubiquitous old blokes watching Bob Katter giving a speech at Jondaryan on *Sky News*.

'Who's that?' asked the old bloke – let's call him Dave.

'That's Bob Katter', I said.

'Where's he talking?' asked Dave.

'Just out of Jondaryan, near the Acland coal mine, not that far from here', I informed him.

'Don't know him. Is he from round here?' drawled Dave.

There's a point to these stories, and it would be well to remember: Queensland is a land of tales, their purpose sometimes not immediately evident. Jasper and Tiffany might think Queensland country folk are as slow as their speech, but they've definitely made a mistake if they do. Laconic country humour is at once rich in self-irony, daring you to take the interlocutor at your own estimation shaped by your own prejudices, and deadly serious about locating both self and other in time and space. If you show respect, you get it back, but you get welcomed as soon as you demonstrate an actual connection to country.

There are some districts in the bush settled by only a few families, and my paternal family comes from one, around Downfall Creek, where Bahnisches, Hoffmans and Stillers worked the land for generations, and were sometimes connected by marriage ties. It was in the graveyard out back of St John's Lutheran Church at Downfall Creek in 2013, another old weatherboard church that the aforesaid families built in the 1930s so they could worship their God on Sundays out of the searing heat, that I realised that Joh's sister, Agneta Bjelke-Petersen, had married Norman Stiller, sometime of Gulugaba, in 1948, and thus Joh was a kind of family connection of mine. It didn't particularly surprise me, nor was I surprised in 1990 when I was invited to dinner with Joh's son-in-law, the Maroochydore pastor, at a friend's mum's place.

Queensland is like that – you're defined by kinship, and by associations, and overlapping circles, which sometimes circle in on themselves in ways that may be surprising to the outsider. Brisbane may be a major metropolis, but pretty much everyone involved in particular everythings knows everyone else, whether it's physical theatre or medieval re-enactment or dissident politics or smells and bells religion. It's hard to hide in Queensland – and while that might mean that outsiders don't easily find acceptance into various magic circles till they prove themselves to a gatekeeper, it also means that there's a certain accountability for what you do. After all, if you intend to continue doing what you do, you'll be doing it with much the same group of people.

YOU'RE NOT FROM ROUND HERE ...

In the middle of the heart-wrenching Queensland floods of 2011, Premier Anna Bligh captured what everyone was thinking when the usually calm and controlled leader almost broke down at one press conference, recalling the damage done to lives and to souls: 'We are Queenslanders. We're the people that they breed tough, north of the border. We're the ones that they knock down, and we get up again.' It might not be spoken very often, and it might be defined negatively, in self-assertion against slurs and 'humour' that dismisses the state as some sort of land of hicks and rednecks, combining stupidity with byzantine politics, but this is a just summation of most Queenslanders' sense of self-identity. So if you're not a Queenslander, it can appear to be a puzzling place, maybe in part because you'll have your puzzlement reflected back to you in the guise of irony. But if you are, you're something else again, from round somewhere. Brisbane is not Cairns, and still less is western Queensland the same place as the tropical north. Everyone is from somewhere up here, and the sum of those somewheres can be an equation that is difficult to solve unless you've lived here, or even better, always lived here.

For those not from round here, it can be a puzzling place, a nowhere-land where the rules are unclear, and things are done differently. Politics seems complicated and corrupt, the coppers menacing, the weather unrelenting – there seems always to be a flood or a cyclone – the sunshine constant – unless interrupted by monsoonal downpours – the topography and foliage different, strange insects ubiquitous, and mangoes everywhere, squishing underfoot in your leafy front yard. Cities seem to be country towns, with no real centre, just inner-city suburbs where decaying Queenslanders sprawl themselves along snaking and windy streets. Small ghost towns recall mining or gold booms long past, and the distances are immense.

If you drive along the Warrego Highway through the Western Downs from Toowoomba to Dalby to Chinchilla to Miles, you are lucky if you get to the next town in an hour, and your mobile reception is bound to drop out about five minutes out of town, unless you have a satellite phone. You might also get stuck behind a truck, or a fleet of four-wheel drives heading off to a coal seam gas construction site. Or you could have a few years back, when the construction and mining booms were booming. Dalby, Chinchilla and Emerald are much quieter places now. Rents are back down to sane levels, but the pubs are no longer full of mining workers on the weekend, and business is slow.

When I last drove from Toowoomba to Chinchilla, it was an awful road and not one that you could overtake on. I don't know if electing an LNP Government in 2012 led to any improvement. Further out west, well, you never get anywhere quickly – ads for motels and tourist attractions in Charleville and Roma start appearing 600 kilometres before you arrive. But news, nevertheless, travels imperceptibly fast along the bush telegraph, a kind of party line that, if you aren't from round here, you can't tune into.

HOW CAN THIS EVEN HAPPEN?

If you did tune into Queensland news recently, it seemed bizarre. The appointment of a Supreme Court Chief Justice leading to a boycott by other judges of his installation ceremony. A librarian locked up in solitary for having a drink with two bikies at a pub. The government sacking a parliamentary committee investigating whether its acting corruption watchdog had lied to parliament. The chair of the ethics committee losing his job because photos of his penis in a glass of wine were released to the press by his disaffected girlfriend. The corruption fighter Tony Fitzgerald denounced by the deputy premier as a dangerous radical. The government planning to pay an Indian company to mine the Galilee basin. Clive Palmer planning to rebuild the *Titanic*. Pauline Hanson running for office – again. An LNP councillor allegedly embezzling the fortune of another councillor, but having a leg-lengthening operation in Siberia, suspected of not wanting to face the courts. Clive Palmer's Coolum resort repopulated with dinosaurs. The Big Pineapple hosting a music festival.

In 2001, I was at a political science conference in Adelaide. All very civilised, as you might imagine. I sat at dinner with colleagues from Adelaide University at a clubhouse (I think) next to the renowned cricket oval, and talk turned to Labor Premier Peter Beattie's prospects at the upcoming state election. Adelaideans, or at least the political science academics among them, were quite aware that there had been a big shemozzle involving electoral malfeasance in the premier's own party, and he had just sacked a number of MPs, despite having only a majority of one in the Legislative Assembly. They assumed that he would lose in a landslide.

'No', I told them, 'he'll win big'. And he did – 66 out of 89 seats. Much more recently, at the end of 2013, I moved to Sydney for a year, in part because the sort of consultancy work I enjoy doing in health workforce policy and health systems management had all dried up, the victim of cuts to budgets in Queensland Health made under the Newman Government, compounded by the abolition of federal health agencies by Tony Abbott's mob. Now domiciled in the dreaded south, I lost count of the number of times I had to explain to southerners the sorts of stuff I've alluded to above, the stuff that the Newman Government was doing on a seemingly daily basis. Progressive media types, radio producers, priests, all sorts of people I spoke to expressed puzzlement – 'How could this happen?' and 'What did it mean?'

2

IS QUEENSLAND DIFFERENT?

" Observers had long noticed Queensland's eccentricity and extremes: Queenslanders had settled in the tropics and the tropics had settled in them. They were, it was said, true inhabitants of the Torrid Zone. In comparison with other Australians, they were considered an odder sort of people – the banana-benders of Banana Land – a heat-stroked and skin-cancered people, dogged, 'unimaginably tough and unimaginably brittle'. They lived under corrugated iron, in houses raised on high, tree-trunk stumps. Though physically proficient, they were both environmentally and historically challenged, rarely looking back and mostly eschewing self-searching criticism. Distance and isolation had sharpened their suspicion of strangers, experts and outsiders. Unrelenting landscapes and the rigours of climate – searing temperatures, droughts or destructive fires, floods and cyclones – bred perseverance but they also fostered obtuse characteristics: the tight-lipped face, the slowed response, the battened-down mind ...

Raymond Evans, *A History of Queensland*, 2007

How could all this happen, and what did it mean? Was Queensland — the state that only a few short years ago gave the nation a progressive governor-general in Quentin Bryce, a progressive prime minister, Kevin Rudd, and a progressive treasurer, Wayne Swan — doomed to revanchist repetitions of the absurd and undemocratic? In answering these and other questions in the aftermath of the January 2015 Queensland State Election, lost resoundingly by the ruling Liberal National Party, which itself had surfed into power on an unprecedented wave a little under three years before, it's well worth revisiting the debates that dominated the Joh era, and tracing how Queensland became assimilated to the craggy jawed visage of Sir Johannes Bjelke-Petersen. This was an era when the state was simultaneously the butt of jokes for its baroque sub-tropical politics and the epicentre of a defiant resistance to derision, a determined desire to take a stand against Canberra. It was as if Queensland was not part of the country, and it was even dubbed a 'Sovereign State' by Joh, who was manoeuvring to make the Queen Queen of Queensland, and asserting that Queensland could 'easily go it alone', leaving all those 'Southern Socialists' to their fate, presumably not a happy one.

In the 1970s, some were determined to deny Queensland's difference. Forces for change emerged in the state's moribund Labor Party during the 1970s and 1980s. Labor's trade union clique, the 'Old Guard', were notorious for spending their days at boozy lunches at the iconic Breakfast Creek Hotel. But a new guard emerged: civil libertarian Senator George Georges, young lawyers like Wayne Goss and Peter Beattie, and progressive western suburbs academics, exemplified by University of Queensland historian Denis Murphy. Veterans of the 1960s' anti-Vietnam War movement, such as English lecturers Dan O'Neill and Carole Ferrier, were also prominent in the struggle.

A caveat was entered in the book *The Deep North* by the then-young philosophy lecturer (and later long-serving MP and Attorney General) Deane Wells, but the consensus among Labor aligned academics and modernisers was that only electoral and institutional manipulation kept the Nats in power. The seeds of a modern 'situation normal' Australian eastern state were still waiting to be watered. The sort of evidence that academic analysts such as Murphy marshalled, sad to say, was somewhat shaped by their own political biases, uniformly Labor. It was wishful thinking rather than objective social science. Murphy would point to the rule of other authoritarian behemoths like Thomas Playford in South Australia, who reigned for 26 years, and point out that Western Australian Premier, Sir Charles Court, had a similar 'develop or bust' mentality, and a similar fondness for mining companies. Bob Askin in New South Wales had been corrupt, or was said to be, and it was notorious that some of the shenanigans the Queensland police indulged in were franchised by cops in

Sydney looking to expand their rackets north of the border. None of this took into account the sorts of factors usually adduced in the 'difference' thesis: the decentralisation; the public role of 'Christian' values and ethics; the great diversity of the state's industries and population centres; the paucity of education and the lower wages, and the absence of capital; and, as historian Raymond Evans has repeatedly emphasised, an economy more reliant on agricultural and mining exports and more subject to boom-and-bust cycles than the nation as a whole. The clincher wasn't delivered by an academic but by a journalist, Peter Charlton, whose *State of Mind: Why Queensland is Different*, published in 1987 as the Joh era was drawing to a tawdry and spectacular close, made the unanswerable point that Joh-style madness had persisted far longer than in other states. The states 'down South' had modernised, while Joh tried to hold back the flood of change and stood for a permanent state of emergency and endless reaction. People had voted for Joh for a reason; they didn't have to. It's also a bit odd that these political scientists and historians apparently failed to see the significance of Queensland's unicameral parliament, the only one of its kind in Australia, and all that implied for the weakening of the rule of law and the dominance of the executive over supine backbenchers and shell-shocked oppositions.

Brisbane, also, is not Queensland, and the state's varied environments and Indigenous peoples were always on the spikes of the developmental pineapple. From sandmining on Stradbroke Island to the preservation of the pristine rainforests of north Queensland, through the rise of coal seam gas and the tearing up of Labor's Wild Rivers legislation by the Newman Government, the environment has been central to Queensland's story. As Evans and other historians of Queensland have emphasised, from the colonial origins of whitefella settlement and dispossession onwards, the environment has figured in the dominant culture as something to be tamed, to be slashed, to be exploited for its agricultural and mining potential. So enduring is this mindset that Peter Beattie's controls on tree clearing were often cited by farmers as horrendous impositions on property rights, and assumed a proportion in state politics quite remarkable given the moderation of the legislation. The last few years of LNP Government saw the dismantling of environmental checks and balances, and constant advocacy of the interests of mining companies over those of local communities and ecologies. Some of the government's first acts were dismantling of climate change projects and agencies. The figurative slash and burn of the early white farmers was back in Newmanland. And we'll be visiting Newmanland later.

LABOR WAS OFTEN A BYSTANDER

Everywhere else in Australia, the Nationals were at best the junior party in coalitions, at worst an irrelevant minor party as in South Australia. In Queensland, the Country Party, and then the Nationals (created up here), ruled the roost, with the Liberals often seemingly irrelevant, and sometimes cast out into the outer darkness of exile on the crossbenches. Three-cornered contests reigned supreme. It's a truism in Australian political analysis to suggest that parties of the centre-right maintained their unity and cohesion more from being against Labor and the union movement than from some animating ideology or body of principles. Politics, it is claimed, was orderly in the past, split along class lines.

If the key divide in Australian politics in the 20th century was between an industrial working class and a capitalist class, that wasn't the picture in the Sunshine State. There was little heavy manufacturing; the unions had their strength in the bush, and the mining; transport and construction industries were more often than not recruiters of short-term contract and seasonal workers, not lifers. Liberals were weak, resting only on the Brisbane legal and medical professions, and big business was always from 'somewhere else' – interstate, if not the American and Japanese capital so warmly embraced by Joh. Rural life was protected by complex marketing and distribution mechanisms, boards, single desks and all the panoply of agrarian socialism, while Queensland was very much a free trade state compared to Victorian industrial protectionism. In this environment, and in a massive landmass overlayed by multiple regional politics (small-scale settlement versus grazing country, red earth versus scrub – a lot more complicated than just urban and rural), we had something like a three-party system, with the Liberals always squeezed in between Labor and Country/National parties, whose respective dominance lasted for decades. Why? More because they represented a certain authoritarian mode of 'strong' governance than because of the social interests on which their bases were built.

Queensland, then, has always been different. Brisbane was a 'branch office' town, which the ambitious sought to or had to leave and where the legal and medical establishments were left to plant the small-l liberal flag on soil never fertile for the sort of social liberalism seen in South Australia under Steele Hall or federally under John Gorton. The Labor Party and the Country Party fought over the scrub and plains of rural Queensland for decades, with the ALP base not being (largely absent) urban manufacturing but out bush – the Australian Workers' Union representing shearers and often miners, and pretty much every worker in the north of the state, the Australian Railways Union the railway workers.

Oddly for those wedded to the claim that Queensland is naturally conservative, the colony briefly had the first Labour Government in the world in 1899, Brisbane saw the world's first general strike in 1912, and early Labor governments under TJ Ryan and 'Red' Ted Theodore charted a path to socialism through intervention in the economy, including the ownership of key state assets. This reformist momentum ran down over time, of course, but Labor's reign was only interrupted by a one-term conservative government from 1929 to 1932, then persisted for another quarter of a century. After the disastrous Labor split of 1957, when Premier Vince Gair was expelled from the party by a temporary coalition of the AWU and the left Trades Hall unions for defying the party platform, the Country Party settled in for a similarly long reign while its city cousins in the Liberals were almost entirely confined to the south east and a smattering of regional cities.

How to explain this 'difference'? Historians, such as Raymond Evans in his distinguished *History of Queensland*, point to the shadows of Brisbane's violent past as a notorious convict settlement, to the legacy of a frontier war that lasted till the 1930s and the effective enslavement of South Sea Islander Kanakas, and to the politics of land grabs that went with the dominance of the squattocracy. Institutions and civil society had always been weak, with the judiciary treated as a field for grace-and-favour appointments, the Upper House abolished by Theodore's Labor Government in 1922, and the police politicised from the get-go. Political scientist Colin Hughes observed that he and his Queensland colleagues needed to study the politics of development and mining approvals rather than ideologies and sociological cleavages.

A recipe, then, for a colourful and populist style of

governance, oriented against Canberra and by a narrative of continuing struggle towards a dour Protestant-promised land of progress. The authoritarianism characteristic of this mission towards the New Jerusalem was as characteristic of a Labor Party forged in the sometimes violent and always hard struggles of shearers and miners, and was only accentuated by Bjelke-Petersen, who increasingly projected himself as a figure co-equal to the state and the State. By 1983, National Party election posters somewhat disturbingly featured Joh's visage superimposed on the map of Queensland with only two words – 'Joh' and 'Queensland', the two clearly considered naturally identical.

This year's Queensland election prompted Jason Wilson, sometime journalism academic hailing from north Queensland and now *Guardian Australia* columnist resident in Oregon, to remark on Twitter that everyone always said that western Sydney was the centre of the Australian political universe, but that most events that sent shockwaves through national politics originated in Queensland. That's something of an impressionistic claim, of course, but it does highlight two things.

First, every ten years or so Queensland exports something or someone remarkable to the rest of the nation – think Joh's assault on Gough Whitlam, the mad Joh for Canberra crusade, Pauline Hanson, Bob Katter, and now Clive Palmer (originally a Victorian, of course, but very much shaped in his character and career by factors and places peculiarly Queensland). Lest it be thought that populist movements and disruptive interventions into the bland verities of the established party system come only from the right, consider KRudd, 'Kevin from Queensland', here to help.

I write these words at Yandina, in a house up on a hill, looking out at Queenslanders nestled among lush native forest, and the looming presence of mountains just beyond town. This is both Clive Palmer's federal electorate of Fairfax and very close to where Kevin Rudd's family farm was located, and just a ten-minute drive from Nambour, where Rudd and Wayne Swan both went to high school. So, then, left as well as right, social democrat as well as reactionary, but all outsized characters, who fit only with difficulty into customary boxes. And this generation was shaped by the same influences – all formed their political views in response to the unprecedented centralism of the Whitlam Government. A young Wayne Swan and a young Kevin Rudd were both in search of a different role for the state, a more expansive and nationwide interventionism, while the young Clive Palmer was on the side of Joh – unrestrained 'free enterprise' was to be preserved at all costs in Queensland against the hordes of southern socialists, exemplified by Gough.

Kevin's troubles as prime minister were not just all about a certain deficiency in management style formed in the autocratic office of Premier Wayne Goss, where he would have given Peta Credlin a run for her money in the command-and-control stakes. He was also a political creature far removed from the Canberra identikit norms, leaving observers bemused by the folksy metaphors and phrases and wondering if everyone from Queensland spoke like him, and his success came precisely from standing apart from and above his party, which is why his party's revenge rebounded so bitterly.

Secondly, it's always as if no one from anywhere else is paying attention, as if these events come out of the blue, as if these personalities, first thought to be objects of provincial curiosity and unable to disturb or influence anything outside Queensland's borders, somehow erupt out of nowhere to seize the national attention and strut the national stage, even for a fleeting moment. Raymond Evans, in a piece for *Griffith Review* published in its *Hidden Queensland* edition, bemoaned the paucity of attention paid to Queensland in histories of Australia. Evans relates that many of the canonical works devote somewhere between 1 and 3 per cent of their content to Queensland, a state which is of course the second largest in landmass and third largest in population. Australia, according to the histories, is New South Wales and Victoria and Canberra, with Tasmania in the mix because of its convict past and maybe a fleeting mention of South Australia as a free settlement. Perhaps, then, it's not just a failure to pay attention, but an unconscious blindness.

Conversely, Queensland itself presented a certain image

to the rest of the nation, whether in the bland celebration of 'progress' inherent in the official histories produced for the state's centenary in 1959 or in its tourist propaganda. You'd have been forgiven for thinking that it was all beaches and pineapples and coalmines. The cringe-worthy segment at the closing of the Glasgow Commonwealth Games had all this in a (pea)nutshell. And if you came here, you'd probably bypass Brisbane and catch a coach or a train straight to one of the coasts – Brisbane being unique among mainland capitals in not having any beaches, except the artificial one in the Southbank parkland across the river from the CBD.

I was always interested to note that interstate friends were constantly inviting me to visit Sydney or Melbourne while never thinking of returning the visit to Queensland, or at least not to Brisbane. Sometimes, God love them, they'd offer to make a detour on the way to the Gold Coast to have a coffee with me and my flatmate at the coffee shop on the corner of Merthyr Road and Moray Street – Brisbane's 'Most Liveable Street 1994' – in New Farm. But mostly, no one would visit unless they were in town for work. One Sydney friend who did come to stay, during a conference, walked with me and a couple of colleagues along the cliff top to the Story Bridge and exclaimed, 'I never knew your city was actually beautiful!'

Peter Beattie once bemoaned the fact that Brisbane had no tourist 'icons', no Harbour Bridge or Opera House. This led, for a while, to proposals to build Big Things on top of Mount Coot-tha overlooking the city, maybe because Queenslanders like to build Big Things – Rockhampton has a Big Cow to surpass even the Big Pineapple. In the end, the then premier settled for designating Grey Street in South Brisbane as 'one of the world's great boulevards', a claim that was widely derided around here, and for good reason. Whatever else Brisbane is, and it's lots of things, it's not Paris, and Peter Beattie was no Baron Hausmann. Don't get me wrong, Peter, we were grateful for the footbridge connecting Gardens and Kangaroo points, and for Suncorp Stadium. Maybe the Story Bridge and the artificial beach at Southbank will just have to do, although you could now no doubt make a case for the spectacular State Library and Gallery of Modern Art.

3
WRITTEN OUT OF *NEIGHBOURS*

In pop culture, I always think of the way that characters are written out of *Neighbours* – 'they moved to Queensland' – as if such a fate implies that no further news would ever be heard from or of such an exile, that there is no returning from this mysterious crossing. The path out of Queensland, whether of political or cultural exile or simply in search for opportunity, is a well-trodden one, but it's as if a move here is a statement that you are irrevocably gone, missing, letters returned to sender. Banjo Paterson captures the cultural representation of this nicely:

> I had written him a letter which I had, for want of better
> Knowledge, sent to where I met him down the Lachlan, years ago,
> He was shearing when I knew him, so I sent the letter to him,
> Just 'on spec', addressed as follows, 'Clancy, of The Overflow'.

QUEENSLAND

And an answer came directed in a writing unexpected,
(And I think the same was written with a thumb-nail
    dipped in tar)
'Twas his shearing mate who wrote it, and verbatim I will
    quote it:
'Clancy's gone to Queensland droving, and we don't
    know where he are.'

In my wild erratic fancy visions come to me of Clancy
Gone a-droving 'down the Cooper' where the Western
    drovers go;
As the stock are slowly stringing, Clancy rides behind
    them singing,
For the drover's life has pleasures that the townsfolk never
    know.

And the bush hath friends to meet him, and their kindly
    voices greet him
In the murmur of the breezes and the river on its bars,
And he sees the vision splendid of the sunlit plains
    extended,
And at night the wond'rous glory of the everlasting stars.

At once, Queensland's a sort of never-never land where one can just disappear, far from 'the foetid air and gritty of the dusty, dirty city', where a metaphysical or ontological change can be wrought upon you; and also a promised land, a nirvana or utopia far removed from urban modernity.

If Raymond Evans is right and there is an unconscious or wilful refusal to know Queensland, then that raises the question of whether the state is somehow ineffable or unknowable. I had a sense of how this might be true after reading Matt Condon's *Brisbane* and Kerryn Goldsworthy's *Adelaide* for an article I never got around to writing, about the differences between the city in which I have lived the overwhelming majority of my life and the city of my birth. Matt Condon's Brisbane is elusive, a child's ever-changing model under the house, compared to Goldsworthy's Adelaide, a bigger grid than Melbourne's with better sightlines, straight roads – you stand on any city street looking along the bitumen, there are no corners or hills and at the end is a mountain.

In Brisbane, you wouldn't have the foggiest where streets go, with hills everywhere and the river appearing unexpectedly, and even worse now with all the tunnels. You think you can see something you're looking for but, as you get closer to it, it turns out to be somewhere other than you expect. I could take you on a walk from the New Farm Bowlo up Bowen Terrace and you'll see the Story Bridge now from one angle, now from another, and lose yourself among the mango trees and the Moreton Bay figs and the palms.

Condon and I are not, by any means, the only writers to recount this phenomenon of perspective. It's not just the topography but also the ephemeral quality of structures – no small cottages firmly set in stone, no sturdy terraces, but weatherboard tin-roofed houses shifting endlessly on their foundations and a city whose landmarks are wont to disappear or reconfigure themselves while you're not noticing. Rodney Hall and Jessica Anderson have also both told of the puzzle of how to find things, unexpected suburb names like Indooroopilly and Woolloongabba that you can never remember how to spell, searches for childhood houses that end in sadness, after backtracks and false clues.

> He watched the trams sliding past, hoping to see one marked New Farm so that he wouldn't have to bother anyone by asking where to catch it. Kalinga, Grange, Ashgrove, Enoggera, Lutwyche (extraordinary names the suburbs here have). He recalled having seen one earlier with the baffling sign: Bulimba Fry, Stafford, Rainworth and Toowong passed up and down the street, but no New Farm. Timidity is the foster-mother of invention: and rather than approach someone, he set off to find out by trial and error. In Queen Street the first tram he saw was the one he wanted.
>
> Rodney Hall, *A Place Among the People*, 1975

Goldsworthy, on the other hand, is able to describe in minute detail the scene of the proclamation of the colony of South Australia as represented in a famous 19th-century painting and to mount an argument about class, race, gender and social relations based almost entirely on the aforesaid painting but also illustrated by a plethora of contemporary and subsequent literary and journalistic accounts. Condon, by contrast, spends much of his book debunking various theories about where John Oxley first landed along the Brisbane River, during the course of which he discovers that nobody actually knows and that the siting of an extremely ugly concrete plaque almost invisible along North Quay was itself a compromise between vociferously contending factions. In his search for the actual site, he ends up in a swamp next to a burnt-out tennis centre in Milton. He notes that nobody actually cares. So for Condon, then, Brisbane is made up by all of its denizens as they go along. And it's not the only place in Queensland where we can say that, although on the coasts pride of place goes to the visions of developers.

TWO COASTS AND MANY DINOSAURS

Guy Rundle recently published a *Quarterly Essay*, *Clivosaurus*, which, among other things, traced Clive Palmer's manifold enterprises and sense of grandiosity to his youth as a dealmaker and log roller on the Gold Coast. Rundle, a long-time visitor to the Gold Coast, captures its ephemerality and sense of shiny emptiness perfectly. A couple of years ago, on my way back to Brisbane from Byron Bay, I noticed from the window of the Greyhound bus the state of decay and disorder many of the 1970s hotels and 'attractions' had fallen into; perhaps the action had moved north from the southern end of the coastal strip. But, flying back into Coolangatta Airport from Singapore recently, I was amazed that the plane had to be towed to the terminal because of 'construction' – a metaphor for the shifting cityscape of the built environment landwards of the beach.

That ugly scenes attend protests against new building projects suggests the politics of redevelopment is often nasty, and very much contested. Labor almost won back the state seat of Broadwater this year because of the sheer atrocity of the scale of waterway destruction about to be inflicted on the district. Mermaid Beach MP Ray Stevens astonished almost everyone with his silent 'bird' dance in response to a reporter's questions over his 'convergence of interest' as both politician and consultant and investor in a development company. *Mermaid Ray*, whose website features 'Ray's Race Tip: Be Nice to Your Mother!' needs to update his blog which, three weeks after Labor formed a government, still proclaimed 'Queensland is Back on Track!' He hasn't crossed the floor; the text still refers to the LNP's 'massive majority', which is no more. Let's not forget that the man whose spectre looms large over the coast, our now old friend Russ Hinze, Minister for Everything under Joh, pioneered both the politics of the land grab and the dodginess that surrounds it. So if the built environment of the Gold Coast resembles something celebrated in the 1970s' promo architecture tome *Learning from Las Vegas*, its social structure seems similarly formless and pliable – the quick road to advancement runs through smarts and swift deals rather than either inherited wealth or constant toil. It does make sense then, that Clive learnt how to be Clive on the Goldie.

Let's not forget either, that Palmer now presides over a dinosaur park and resort on the Sunshine Coast, minutes away from slumbering Mount Coolum. The Gold Coast has always been *sui generis*, even in Queensland terms. Plots hatched there – like the madness of the 'Joh for PM' crusade cooked up in concert with Mike Gore and the 'white shoe brigade' of property developers – have tended to run aground or implode. Maybe because the Goldie, a promised land in one sense, has always been a nowhere land, home to people from elsewhere. It feels simultaneously like not-Queensland and hyper-Queensland. That's its utopic and its dystopic quality. Crime stats, particularly those involving violence and guns, are disproportionately bad on the Gold Coast compared to the rest of the state, and Campbell Newman's war on bikies may, in one sense, have been an instance of something that seemed like an overreaction everywhere else.

The Sunshine Coast couldn't be more different, with the exception of the glitzy high-rise and nightclub beachfront of Mooloolaba. Coolum, Peregian and Marcoola beaches are sleepy, Caloundra has more bustle, and Noosa is Noosa – either the Toorak of the North or the Byron Bay of Queensland, depending on your taste and the state of the economy. Buderim is ginger and bookshops and Peter Slipper's hideaway house. The south of the Sunshine Coast from Buddina down to Caloundra is pretty much all non-stop featureless 1980s housing estates but the north is brush and tea trees, segueing into rainforest. Proverbially, and as I was told once by a retired senior sergeant of police at Maroochydore over prawns and XXXX, the refugees from Jeff Kennett's Victoria all went bust after buying low-lying land on the flood plains unawares. They had stars in their eyes, dreams of canals and subdivisions, but forgot to check the flood maps. I don't know if that's true, but it captures the culture of the place – you win in politics on the Sunshine Coast by promising not to be the Gold Coast. Clive ran into much trouble with the council and with locals precisely because the dinosaurs and the land grabs were more Surfers Paradise than Sunshine Coast. In the hinterland, as we've seen, this is Kevin Rudd country, too, in vibe if not in votes, although the old timber-logging town of Eumundi has had an agreeably New Age makeover (and yet more bookshops). The Gold Coast, despite the presence of three universities to the Sunshine Coast's one, is not noted for bookshops.

As a bred-if-not-born Queenslander myself, I'm much fonder of the Sunny Coast than the Cold Ghost. There's a local identity here, and roots laid down. Sure, there are people from 'not round here', but old British migrants drinking themselves silly at the bowls club fit in with local folkways well. There was never any heavy industry, the banana and strawberry farms are mostly gone, and I've never been able to figure out while passing through what most people do for a living in places like Buddina. Maybe the interspersed bottlos and fundamentalist churches amidst the brick-box houses provide a clue, but I'm not sure. I'm being a little unfair, as the Sunshine Coast Council is working hard to promote big projects and major employers, often with the assistance of state government. The Sunshine Coast University Hospital, the medical facility that the LNP tried to privatise even before it was finished, springs to mind. I do know – just as with other more northerly districts along the sprawling Queensland coastline – average incomes are low. If you drive from Buderim down to Maroochydore, every second house seems to offer knife sharpening or fresh fruit or some other good or service, usually via a hand-painted sign.

Further north, particularly in the hinterland, 'all night Shiva worship' notices can be found next to old country wooden churches and pubs, and Ayurvedic medicine and crystal shops abound. There are no doubt dreams dreamt here, but not the sorts of grand ones Clive envisages, which may account for the puzzlement Rundle describes at the bizarre PUP open show Palmer organised in 2014 at his Coolum resort, to give the locals a taste of his politics as well as entertain them with Elvis impersonators. As Rundle also notes, not many of the voters of Fairfax actually cast a first preference vote for PUP in the person of the sometime Professor Palmer from Bond University. Let's recall, again, that Kevin Rudd, independent Peter Wellington, who delivered government to state Labor in hung parliaments in both 1998 and 2015, and Clive all overlap geographically around the Sunshine Coast hinterland. Things are not, perhaps, as they seem.

IS QUEENSLAND KNOWABLE?

He's probably little remembered now, but Vance Palmer, a distinguished Australian essayist and novelist and one half of one of our most famous literary partnerships alongside his wife Nettie, wrote an incredible trilogy called *Golconda*, following the fortunes of miner then Labor politician Macy Donovan from his beginnings as a union representative in the eponymous mining camp to his eventual premiership and personal implosion. Loosely based on 'Red' Ted Theodore's life, the trilogy adopts something of a socialist-realist style, not without echoes of Joseph Conrad, although with only one sea voyage. *Golconda*, the first novel, only really approaches lyricism when it describes the huge rock, Mount Isa in reality, waiting to be scoured and extracted, a parable of mining, human power and nature.

Golconda, in reality, is an abandoned fort in India,

once the site of legendary diamonds. In the novel, despite the material weight of the mountain, Golconda functions as a sort of mythical template, the object and subject of dreams and striving. Gougers who flock to stake out their claims are as likely to abandon their camp at a moment's notice and rush to a rumoured goldfield. They'll be helped along by the mining companies, keen to get their impersonal hands on the leases where the old blokes have been mining by hand. The only gouger who holds out, the Old Testament prophet lookalike Christy Baughan, dreams of an intentional community, a recreation of the aforementioned William Lane's dream that soured. But it's the companies and the unions who become fixtures, and the promises of both untold wealth and realised utopia become mythical. Go back there a few years later, and myth has been domesticated into straight streets, a schoolhouse and a railway station. One day all will be abandoned, as empty as the Golconda Fort.

The two sequels, *Seedtime* and *The Big Fellow*, are set largely in Brisbane, but you hardly get a sense of the place. Place only comes alive when we're up in Caloundra, where Macy revisits his obsessive love for the sculptress Neda, herself a worker of the earth and rocks, just as the miners are. If you read Jack Lindsay's memoir, *Life Rarely Tells*, writing of his Edwardian childhood in Brisbane, coincident in time with Macy's early years, there's an exceptionally strong sense of place around Parliament House, boarding houses a bit like Macy's on North Quay, and mysterious Chinese women. But it's impossible to go and find, should you wish, an intensely realised description of a place whose traces have all now disappeared, just as David Malouf's *12 Edmondstone Street* has now been swallowed whole by a TAFE college.

In *The Big Fellow*, Neda turns out to have found success in Prague, a city where every move Kafka made is immortalised in stone or on a plaque. Compare David Malouf, the most famous writer Brisbane has produced, who grew up in and wrote a whole book about his childhood house; it's gone and the suburb isn't really called South Brisbane any more, the nearby station isn't called Vulture Street, and on the other side of the river Brunswick Street station has become Fortitude Valley. In Prague, streets change their names with changes in political regime, but monuments to the past are constants. Johnno and Dante would find it hard to find their way around Brisbane now. The trams are gone too, the lines ripped up in 1969 in the name of progress after a large part of the fleet burnt in a fire in 1962. Brisbane is prone to conveniently timed fires, the more so when development is halted by heritage laws. How can we know somewhere that is never constant? Is Queensland more a state of mind than anything else?

There are some constants, though. In Andrew McGahan's *Last Drinks*, the anti-hero, George Verney, fleeing the ruin of his life as the Fitzgerald Inquiry sees it come crumbling down, halts just north of the New South Wales border, unable to leave Queensland, even as it changes beneath his feet in a flash and all his values are turned upside down. Verney is a character motivated by upheaval and personal crisis mirroring the political crisis of the fall of the National Party regime, but any Queenslander will tell you the state is a bit like Franz Kafka's Prague – once it has its claws in you, it's impossible to really leave, and you will always dream of returning. And wherever you go, you will meet people from Queensland you know. It's a law of the universe.

In Rosa Praed's *Outlaw and Lawmaker*, published in 1893 but set in the thinly disguised 'Leichardt's Land' of the 1860s, the outlaw character is also a lawmaker, simultaneously the police minister and the most feared bushranger, so effectively in charge of hunting himself down – connecting to what corrupts. And the 'Leichardt's Town' of the 1860s, where Elsie Valliant makes her home at Emu Point, is a small stage on which all the players know each other. So maybe not much has changed, really. That's also an impression you get when you pore over, as I once did, Hansards from the 1890s. The same names as those that National Party ministers and MPs bear ninety years later are there: Glassons and Gunns.

A COOK'S TOUR

Four final occurrences finished Drayton's hopes. It lost its court hearings, the first municipal council split into violent factions and disgraced itself, even by Queensland standards, with a series of outrageous and ludicrous meetings, the first pastoral shows were held in Toowoomba, and the final humiliation, on 1 May 1867 the railway from Ipswich reached Toowoomba's heart and subsequent branches bypassed Drayton altogether.

Thereafter Drayton remained an irritating boil on Toowoomba's neck, feeling neglected by its neighbour's representatives, recalling the glories of pre-Separation days, agitating for a railway deviation (which they finally achieved in 1906 when it was too late for the town to survive as an independent entity) and gradually declining into a sleepy two-pub nucleus for numerous smallholders until their little farms were swallowed up by the advancing suburbs of the larger city.

DB Waterson, *Squatter, Selector and Storekeeper*,
1968

Before the colony of Queensland was proclaimed in 1859, from the balcony of what is now the Deanery of Brisbane's St John's Anglican Cathedral, whose spires rise above the

Valley end of Ann Street, the favoured name for the separated colony was Cooksland. It's said that Queen Victoria came up with the name that endured, but the machinations that led to the detachment from New South Wales of the then District of Moreton Bay all the way up to the Torres Strait Islands often revolved around its borders. Maximal claims took the border all the way down to New England, encompassing Armidale. Minimal ones would have seen the border drawn just south of Brisbane.

As with federation, and as with election campaigns subsequently, folk north of Brisbane, or at least urgers and the politically ambitious, were often agitating for their own governments, and schemes were schemed, and maps made up. Labor Premier Ned Hanlon, justifying additional representation for remote districts, introduced into parliament in 1947 the bill that first gave the state electoral malapportionment, and mused that had Western Queensland become a state, Longreach would have been a thriving metropolis of 80,000. Back in 1859, Ipswich had a claim to being the capital, and because its tiny electorate of squatters reliably returned conservative members, it was in with a chance. By an 'oversight', the new colony ended up with such a restrictive franchise that electorates had around 100 or fewer voters. Someone, having made a slip and got the year when New South Wales' law continued to be applied wrongly, thus wiped out manhood suffrage with an inkblot. It was a bad start. 'One vote one value' was a concept that came very late to Queensland elections, not being achieved until Wayne Goss' administration 130 years later.

What eventually coalesced as a state where residents of the north can describe Brisbanites as southerners was always an uncertain and shifting landscape of the mind, difficult to encompass and circumscribe as an entity, even as a geographical space. Tourism, we are told, is now one of the state's 'pillars', and no doubt there are many rational and logical routes planned out via guide books, but it would be hard to design a Cook's Tour of the state that really covered it all. So if my Cook's Tour starts on a bus ride from Byron Bay up through the south of the Gold Coast and skips Brisbane for the northernmost reaches of the Sunshine Coast, it then travels back in time and recalls the mid-1990s when my friends and I, poor students stuck for things to do, were in the habit of visiting country races, notably at Esk where those quintessential Queenslanders, the Kransky Sisters, famously hail from.

One Saturday, at least I think it was Saturday, we conceived the mad project of trying to visit all the race meetings in South East Queensland on one day. This entailed going initially to Kilcoy, about two hours from Brisbane, where the first nag I bet on jumped the fence and literally darted off to freedom, having thrown her rider, and where you are welcomed into town by a statue of a Yowie – no, I don't know the story. Then back, way up the range to Toowoomba, and to the greyhounds, after some lunatic in an old Datsun has tried to play chicken on the steep incline up Murphy's Creek Road. Of course, we had to abandon the goal of making Redcliffe, just north of Brisbane but decidedly not Brisbane, as the locals won't hesitate to emphasise – I wonder if the railway line that's been promised at every state election since 1921 might change this. So we settled down in a pub on Ruthven Street, I can't remember which one, for a night of karaoke consisting mainly of Chisel songs. Lord only knows at this distance in time how we managed to afford beer after backing so many long shots. I think we were sympathetic to Neal Cassady's cry in Jack Kerouac's *On the Road* at this point: 'Why all this mad running around?' You can be a dharma bum in Queensland, too, I'd suggest.

Toowoomba, the largest non-capital city in Australia on the west of the Great Divide, and about an hour and a half's drive from Brisbane if the traffic is good (which it rarely is up the notoriously dangerous range crossing), was a lot more country in those days, not yet graced by either Asian or Middle-Eastern students studying at the University of Southern Queensland or Sudanese refugees, and with cattlemen in big hats a more common sight, and still with its own department stores like Piggott's and McKinney's. It's a lovely town, quite different in its residential and commercial and public architecture from Brisbane, quite art deco in places, and reminiscent of Armidale in some ways, with tree-lined streets heading up the range, and some fascinating colonial architecture, some of which strangely echoes Byzantium. The Prague of the South, I like to call it, to general bafflement. The annual Flower, Food and Wine Festival, held in Queens Park under ancient trees on a night so clear you can properly see the Southern Cross, and USQ's Shakespeare in the Park, are both wonderful events; and the Empire Theatre, built in 1911, is a thing of beauty too. The Camerata of St John's, a celebrated chamber orchestra, visits St Luke's on Ruthven Street as well as the Cathedral back in Brisbane.

My paternal grandmother lived in Toowoomba as a young girl, working in service to a bourgeois family and, as family lore has it, becoming a socialist and a lifelong Labor voter as a result. Certainly at the booth at which my grandparents voted on the Western Downs there was always one vote not cast for the Country Party, although nobody ever knew who cast it. Toowoomba grew rapidly in the late 19th century, enriched by grazing wealth, and eclipsed its poor cousin Drayton, where a local history remarks council meetings were absurd, violent and turbulent even by Queensland standards. These days, you could drive out towards Crows Nest, stop for the best gravy in the world at the Cabarlah pub, and then shop for German cuckoo clocks. If you take off for Dalby, as I did when I was researching coal seam gas, you could share a beer or two with a garbage contractor, or you could tip your hat to an Indigenous woman crossing the bridge over Myall Creek, and note her surprise at politeness from someone wearing an Akubra. This is my Cook's Tour, a tour of the mind, and others would end up elsewhere.

I can almost take you in imagination up to Cape York, because I was close to an Indigenous woman at uni who hailed from there, and assure you that many Murris are no fans of Noel Pearson, despite what you might have read in *The Australian*. We could visit the harbour of Gladstone, whose port, now staying in public hands under Labor, is expanding rapidly because of coal seam gas exports, where you might even see dead fish wash up on the shore, or so a Marist priest told me. Or we could recreate a high school tour and drive all the way to Mount Isa, circling back to Golconda of legend.

Everyone's Queensland is a different one and, for many, there's a search, mad and frenzied or otherwise, for a promise that remains unrealised. The thing about progress or the modern is it's always just out of your grasp, and the thing about utopias is that they are literally nowhere.

So can you know Queensland? Mine will be different from other Queenslanders'. Like the gougers in Golconda skipping camp on the whisper of gold or me and my mates dashing around the country race meetings, sometimes we're all running around like mad things in search of the next dream, the next promising place. Sometimes, it proves illusory, a dream unrealised, and it's best to settle for karaoke in the pub. Or rest somewhere in a deckchair on your own back deck, watching the mangoes fall, and waiting for the storm to hit. I think the tension between movement and fixity somehow defines something core to Queensland's spirit, to its being. And William Lane was offered a land grant by the colonial government to build his utopia, but nevertheless felt impelled or compelled to run to Paraguay instead. The spirit of escape is strong too, although you can never really leave in spirit.

4

GOOD COFFEE COMES TO BRISBANE

So what of the political history of a state where a premier could effectively be put on trial in an AWU meeting room with a noose suspended over the speaker's podium? Vince Gair was the Australian Labor Party's last Queensland premier before Wayne Goss, and briefly the Queensland Labor Party's only premier after the split. As we've seen, the Queensland Split was less about the Movement and the groupers and more a trial of strength between a united union movement and the majority of the cabinet, ostensibly over the granting of three weeks' annual leave to workers and, significantly, the independence from government dictation of the University of Queensland. Gair stood firm on his principle of parliamentary sovereignty, and faced what was effectively a show trial in front of the Queensland Central Executive of the ALP, meeting at the AWU's headquarters, Dunstan House in Queen Street, the true centre of power at the other end of town from the stately Parliament House in George Street.

For a few years, the Queensland Labor Party, the faction that followed Gair out of the party, including the entire cabinet bar Deputy Premier Jack Duggan, tried to maintain the claim that it was a realistic pretender to office. Although the ALP was fatally wounded and would not look competitive again for a long time, most QLP members lost their seats or hung on as independents after the 1960 and 1963 elections. With the once omnipotent ALP now reduced to a shadow of its former self on the opposition benches, the Country Party reigned supreme in coalition with the Liberals. The remnants of the QLP eventually collapsed into the welcoming arms of the Democratic Labor Party, and Gair went to the federal senate. His last hurrah was his appointment as Ambassador to Ireland, a move engineered by Gough Whitlam to deliver Labor a crucial senate seat, only to be outsmarted by Joh Bjelke-Petersen.

The new premier in 1957, the Country Party's Frank Nicklin, had admitted as recently as 1955 that it was unlikely that Labor would ever lose office. Artie Fadden, a Queenslander and the combative federal leader of the Country Party, had to point out to him that the conservatives could form government. Probably to Nicklin's surprise, he found himself on the government benches, after first thinking of supporting Vince Gair's continuation in power. Although outvoted by the two Labor parties in the

1957 election, they were rarely troubled by the opposition throughout the decade to come.

If Queensland largely slept politically under the paternalistic reign of Frank Nicklin, often pictured with his pipe in mouth, the signs of change that heralded what later became known as the 'sixties' – culturally, an era that perhaps lasted from The Beatles to its self-immolation with Weather Underground and Charles Manson, but with after-effects lasting until punk – were nevertheless evident, at least in Brisbane. Parliamentary Labor was still old men in serge suits, but the campuses and the rusting weatherboard suburbs of West End and New Farm were starting to burn with a different fire.

West End became the home of Greeks, with the mansions of the late 19th-century haute bourgeoisie gazing down on the concreted front yards and cafes from the ridge of Highgate Hill above, while the Italians ruled the roost in the workers' cottages north of Brunswick Street in New Farm. Largely of Calabrian and Sicilian origin, some immigrants coming south from the Innisfail canefields, Italian folk introduced Brisbane to pizza, pasta, good coffee and bocce. If New Farm was about hedonism and the thrill of danger, West End was all stronger coffee and politics.

The coppers kept themselves busy making new links with another offshoot of postwar immigration – Italian crime families, whose gambling joints were displacing the department stores, which were eclipsed by suburban 'shoppingtowns' in the Valley. Contending crime families, of whom the Bellino brothers were to become the most prominent during the 1970s, colonised rambling Queenslanders in Kangaroo Point for brothels, where the Woolloongabba CID often took its take in kind. At the same time, older anarchist and left-wing Catholic currents and tendencies, often unified around bookshops and coffee shops, were starting to coalesce with national and international movements both of opinion and of style. If, as Gerard Lee suggests, the beatniks had only a remote echo in the sleepy and then largely treeless streets of Brisbane, and if the hippies were either across the border in northern New South Wales or way up north in the rainforest, the more political aspects of sixties' counter-culture were making a home in the metropolis.

Rock music burst on the scene in the late 1950s, to the annoyance of the police who often broke up groups of fans queuing outside Festival Hall in town along Elizabeth Street. Anything new, and particularly anything American, was suspect, unless it was mining capital, skyscrapers and freeways. Bob Dylan once came to town and remarked that progress appeared to have left the state behind. Brisbane began to trash its heritage, with stately colonial edifices giving way to square towers and sleepy Queenslander houses disappearing under a blight of roads and concrete blocks. The Bellevue Hotel on Albert Street, a gracious reminder of earlier colonial gentility, lasted until 1978, when it was demolished by the notorious Deen Brothers. But the wrecking ball had been flying from the 1960s, with the Town Hall no longer the tallest tower on the skyline.

IT'S THE SIXTIES, STREET MARCHES ARE ALL THE RAGE

The University of Queensland, on a pocket of land at St Lucia surrounded on two sides by one of the river's many snake-like bends, was an unlikely site for dissent to bubble up. Its very existence was questioned by some Labor MPs, including 'Red' Ted Theodore at its inception, and it had taken a long time to find a permanent home away from its original temporary digs in Old Government House on Gardens Point. Premier Forgan Smith laid the foundation stone of the sandstone quad in 1937, looking rather uncomfortable in academic gown and cap. The Forgan Smith Building, the cornerstone of the quad, wasn't complete until 1952, although the university moved to the site donated by the prominent Catholic Mayne family in 1947.

Busts of Aristotle and Aquinas may have graced the Forgan Smith Building's imposing facade, but the university was oriented largely to pragmatic and technical pursuits – engineering and geology and agricultural science being more valued than the Faculty of Arts, with its classical and literary studies. Photos from 1965 of the cavernous main refectory – much later to be a noted venue for the pioneering indie FM 4ZZZ station's 'joint effort' concerts that spawned many of the 'Brisbands' Andrew Stafford writes of in *Pig City*, to the displeasure of both the university registrar and the good burghers of Dutton Park across the river, as noise travelled – show masses of young men in long-sleeved shirts and ties.

As elsewhere, the demands of a technocratic and nascent knowledge economy expanded higher education, even if the late advance of any form of post-primary education aside from the grammar schools and elite Catholic schools meant that the university still only had 6000 students in the late 1960s – not a single state high school had been opened in Brisbane for 20 years before 1952, despite a rapidly expanding population. It was remarkable then, that a full 3000 of those students marched to town, only to be assaulted by police, at the height of the Vietnam War protests. Figures like Brian Laver and Mitch Thompson, young academics Dan O'Neill, Carole Ferrier and Peter Wertheim, were to found a long tradition of libertarian and socialist-left protest and, in Laver's case, an anarchist ghetto in West End, centred on Emma's Bookshop and the remarkable *West End Neighbourhood News*, probably the country's most politicised local rag while it lasted. But 1960s' idealism, in these heady days, met the immovable forces of the Country Party and the police force. There were no votes from enlightened lawyers south of Coolangatta, but there were votes aplenty in the bush, where long-haired radicals hitchhiked at their own risk.

HE WAS JOE BEFORE HE BECAME SIR JOH

When Nicklin's successor Jack Pizzey suddenly died of heart failure after a mere six months in office, on 31 July 1968, a week went past when Deputy Premier and Liberal Leader Sir Gordon Chalk allegedly manoeuvred to take the top job, some said even considering joining the Country Party. Chalk was the Member for Lockyer, a country constituency, and was more popular and more experienced than the Country Party's deputy, Joh Bjelke-Petersen. Petersen, as he was then known, had been a minister only since 1963, despite having entered parliament in 1947. Petersen had been a lay preacher in his youth, and my father remembers sermons Joe preached on circuit through country parishes. A self-made man, son of a pastor who had emigrated from New Zealand and taken badly to farming due to ill health and 'nerves', Petersen junior had expanded into crop dusting and land clearing as well as peanut farming. A keen pilot, Petersen was seen as a 'wowser' and often taunted by Labor members, usually fond of a tipple in the House.

Petersen was known for his jeremiads against socialism as much for his occasional tilts at his own side of politics, and his elevation to the ministry was as much to contain a troublemaker within the tent as to reward performance. Joh seized his opportunity and built up a store of favours as the Minister for Works and Housing – a bridge here, and a school hall there – all of which could be called in when he wanted to ascend to the premiership. And ascend he did, although his early years in office were marred by inept attempts to soften his image – posing with a racehorse and having the more roustabout Minister for Mines Ron Camm shout the bar on his behalf. In the early days of his rule, his first name was often spelt 'Joe' to avoid the 'ethnic' orthography of 'Joh', and to make the lay preacher seem more of a man of the people. But he seemed very much a man behind the times, a throwback to an earlier era.

Joh's Country Party administration, rebranded as the National Party, steadied its shaky start in 1973 when a 'state of emergency' was declared for the Springbok Tour, and country cops charged demonstrators, many familiar faces from the Vietnam era, in Brisbane's Albert Park. Rewarded with by-election victories, including the election in inner city Merthyr of 'Shady' Don Lane, former special branch detective and later to be jailed after the Fitzgerald Inquiry, 'Jackboots' Bjelke had found a formula for electoral success, aided and abetted by the notorious electoral zonal system or gerrymander. In 1974, the 'bible bashing bastard' outsmarted Gough Whitlam, reduced state Labor to a cricket team of 11 members, and sailed on triumphant throughout the 1970s, banning street marches and bulldozing the state's heritage and environment in the sacred cause of progress. Stern and strong, tongue-tied but folksy, Bjelke-Petersen reigned over a state whose foundational legacies had been decentralisation, an economy oriented to agricultural and then mining exports, and a weak urban professional class, as well as a largely rural working-class union base in the Australian Workers' Union.

It's often not realised that Queensland in the 1970s and 1980s had something more akin to a three-party system than a straight fight between Labor and the Coalition, as we've seen. That's because the Coalition here was even more shaky than elsewhere – with the Liberals often generating a 'ginger group' in parliament concerned to speak up for accountability, due process and often, the environment. Led informally by Terry White and then Angus Innes, both urban professionals and both later to lead the decimated party after Joh destroyed it in 1983, the 'trendies' were always in a state of extreme tension with the state of authoritarianism favoured by the Joh Nationals. Liberal treasurers Sir Gordon Chalk, Sir William Knox and Dr Llew Edwards had to straddle a rickety fence between loyalty to Joh and their own backbench and party organisation, and three-cornered contests were never absent. As Joh himself said more than once, bad things awaited those who tried to straddle fences. Political scientist Paul Reynolds' biography of post-Joh Premier Mike Ahern reveals periodic secret deals between Labor and the Nationals to marginalise the Liberals, and between the Libs and Labor to chip away at the Nats' dominance. So, elections were more often than not fights between the Liberals and Nationals, after the party reinvented itself to appeal more broadly outside the bush.

The Labor Party was usually trapped in the headlights, more spectator of the internecine warfare between the governing parties than contender for government itself. Joh's push for Brisbane territory, aided and abetted by the self-destructive instincts of the Liberals (although it should be recognised that White and Innes and others stood up bravely for liberal principles in a manner unrecognisable among their ideological descendants like George Brandis), was always supported by the Nationals' machine under Sir Robert Sparkes. In 1983, the Nats gained power in their own right through the agency of the defection of two Liberal ministers, Brian Austin and Don Lane, both later jailed. After a promising Nat performance in a by-election for Clayfield in 1977, contested by the party secretary Mike Evans, and a disappointing one in Sherwood the following year, Mrs Flo Bjelke-Petersen then won a swag of Brisbane votes to take a federal senate spot off the Liberals in 1980. Flo's appeal, with her famous pumpkin scones and grandmotherly folksy charm, was much broader in the bush. A swathe of urban seats were captured by the Nationals in 1983 and 1986, often ones like Mount Gravatt that had a strong fundamentalist Christian constituency.

GROWING UP IN JOHBURG

Punk hit Brisbane like no other city in Australia. The tentacles that grew out of New York and London from the musical explosion of 1976 affected the receptive waiting enclaves in each major city around the globe in varying ways. As the music and images of the Ramones, Patti Smith, early Pere Ubu, Television and the Sex Pistols were heard and seen, bands formed, systems started and the word spread. Brisbane was different, for two main reasons: we had Bjelke-Petersen and The Saints. Bjelke-Petersen represented the kind of crypto-fascist, bird-brained conservatism that every punk lead singer in the world could only dream of railing against. His use of a blatantly corrupt police force, and its heavy-handed response to punk, gave the scene a political edge largely absent in the other states. And The Saints were the musical revolutionaries in the city's evil heart.

> Robert Forster, 'Tales from Pig City', *The Monthly*, September 2007

I was born in 1968, shortly before Joh took the reins of power. He was the only premier I knew until I was almost 20. Like many other Queenslanders of all ages, on family holidays down south when I was a teenager I breathed a sigh of relief when the car crossed the New South Wales border. The air felt freer, and it was a journey many older youngsters had taken before me, exiled from the Sunshine State, driven out or unable to live as they chose in the state's increasingly oppressive atmosphere.

Publicans could legally refuse service to anyone they considered a 'pervert', a measure largely targeted at gay men, but flexible enough to encompass anyone different. Books, movies and plays were censored, and it wasn't unknown for cops to shut down gigs. Stories of interstate musos visiting and being hassled by cops are legion. There was nearly always a 'state of emergency' declared for some reason or another, and the notorious *Gaming, Vagrancy and Other Offences Act 1936* banned fortune telling and going about at night in shoes without a leather sole. Whether or not there were many arrests for this latter heinous crime, the scope of this legislation, and so much other public order law, allowed anyone to be detained on almost any excuse at any time. Institutionalised paranoia reigned, and it really did feel like the walls had eyes and phones had ears, as the Parameters sang in their 1983 tune 'Pig City'. We were all behind the Banana Curtain.

As a young public servant, back in the time when you could get a full-time job as a clerk, I spent my days during the SEQEB (South East Queensland Electricity Board) strike of 1985, when the power was off more often than not, in the cellar of the Treasury Building working by candlelight, and my nights on the front porch with another candle, sipping whiskey. On weekends, I attended meetings of the Queensland Coalition for Democratic Rights, or marched in the streets. I remember the ritual that went on after a street march: another procession up to the watch house to bail comrades out, after a collection was taken at the pub – the Criterion in Adelaide Street or the QIT Campus Club at Gardens Point being favoured venues.

These were also years, as I was to discover in 1987, that anyone involved in left-wing politics or the civil liberties movement could expect a knock on the door at 6 am and a visit from special branch detectives with a dodgy warrant, who would look at photos of parties and ask who was and who was not a communist or active in dissent. It wasn't clear what would happen to you if you refused to answer, but stories of activists being held without charge for days and beaten by cops periodically appeared in publications like *The Cane Toad Times* and the UQ Union paper *Semper*. Telephone books cushioned the blows, and magistrates never disbelieved police anyway. On Labour Day in 1986, when the march was over and unionists, socialists, Murris, feminists and Labor members gathered at Albert Park in Spring Hill for sangers and beers, I spotted Don Lane, then a Minister of the Crown, hiding behind the bushes with a long-lens camera taking photos of revellers. Rallies in King George Square would regularly see brown-shirted special branch cops, their undercover skills needing some work, act as provocateurs. To the question from the fortysomething detective, masquerading as a perpetual student, 'What do you study, comrade?' the correct answer was always, 'Law, Senior Sergeant'.

The patriarch himself was known for his good manners,

quite the Lutheran gentleman, despite the animosity he showed to any who did not walk the true path. I waited on him, a casual gig, at a table under a huge marquee on the forecourt of the Art Gallery, overlooking the river. The occasion was the birthday of future exile Christopher Skase, who had just bought Channel Ten and built himself an atrociously brash mansion near the top of Hamilton Hill. That did not endear him to his neighbours, the scions of the squattocracy, the Anglican Archbishop and the medical and legal establishments. Cut off from political power, Brisbane's old rich on the heights overlooking the river maintained a social exclusivity where you would have to endure three generations before anyone in an interloping family received an invitation to tennis or for a gin and tonic. Skase probably didn't care. He was happy dining with National Party ministers and other arriviste business types, property developers notable among them, who were flocking to the Sunshine State for a quick buck, facilitated by paper bags full of a lot of bucks.

At the time, Alan Bond was taking on his own unions at the XXXX brewery down the river at Milton, and was already planning his eponymous university. Fast money, boom times, rivers of gold for the National Party machine which spewed out imperial honours and development approvals in return. The Joe Petersen of 1968 had now morphed into Sir Johannes Bjelke-Petersen, having given himself a knighthood in 1984. Significantly, according to some, he fumbled and dropped the medallion when it was handed to him by the Queen at Buckingham Palace.

THE MINISTER FOR CORRUPTION TAKES A TUMBLE

If you go downtown, just beware
There's a demonstration in the square
The boys in blue are everywhere

See the blacks in the park
Hear the doors slam, hear the dogs bark
They're keeping the city safe after dark

The minister for corruption's working late
He wants a piece of the action in Race 8
No s.p. here, he's ringing interstate

The blacks in Aurukun have to go
To keep big business on the go
While Joh gets shares in Comalco

Who was the bagman, who was the hitman
Who were the frontmen, who were the big men
In the National scam?

Hello, hello, is that you dear?
What's that clicking noise I hear?
Walls have eyes and phones have ears

Go to a dance to have some fun
Here come the boys with their dogs and guns
They don't like punks, run, Johnny, run

Who's that knocking at the door?
At 6 am it must be the law
Right, you know what we're looking for

A state of emergency for the 'Boks
And then to show the workers who's boss
You think you've got rights, they're already lost

So you don't want to know, you've heard it before
But if you cop this lot, you'll sure get more
Where to now from '84?

The Parameters, 'Pig City' (lyrics by Tony Kneipp),
1983

As the 1986 election approached, particularly when Sir Roderick Proctor, one of a coterie of National Party knights, admitted to reporter Quentin Dempster that he had paid a hundred grand for his, we dared to hope. But

Dempster was treading a lonely and courageous path, and most Queenslanders seemed to continue to slumber. Labor's unconvincing champion, the decent but uninspiring former electrician, Neville 'Call Me Nev' Warburton, went down to defeat, actually losing two seats. Still, it was the first election I voted in and I drank XXXX at a mate's place in Mount Gravatt with some anticipation, before consoling myself with the thought that the Bjelkemander, an epithet applied to this state's 'zonal system', which awarded country voters a franchise worth three times as much as those in Brisbane, made change impossible anyway.

Not a happy thought, and nor was the hangover pleasant, but young hearts recover quickly, and as a first-year student at university, having cut short my unspectacular career as a public servant, political activism beckoned again. These were the years when you could hang around the 4ZZZ studio on campus at any hour of the day or night, drinking and chatting with Murris, or listening as one of the volunteer journos rang Joh at Bethany. The premier's home number was on speed dial, if such a thing existed on the Telecom standard analogue phones of the era. Joh would always answer, never too busy to have a spray at students, communists, the Labor Party, all his enemies, always the same enemies.

By 1987, I was living in a ramshackle share house on Kangaroo Point, a stone's throw away from the river. Brisbane was still the proverbial country town in those days, and I well remember a cow or two grazing on a farm next to the Catholic Church in Kenmore where I grew up, and playing in bush only a few streets away from 1960s/1970s suburbia. You could live cheaply, and my flatmates and I were bordered on one side by a bunch of bikies who used to like to play guitar on their deck, and on the other by a disused factory where strange things, probably involving drug manufacturing, used to occur in the wee hours. We were normally up watching old black-and-white movies on TV, so we knew. One night we were shocked, watching 'The Moonlight State', the notorious episode of *Four Corners* broadcast on 11 May, wherein reporter Chris Masters blew the whistle on the links between the police, organised crime and the National Party Government, leading in quick succession to the Fitzgerald Inquiry, called by Deputy Premier Bill Gunn in Joh's absence. In a real way, this one TV show was the beginning of Joh's downfall.

When Joh did come crashing down, it was as quick as the Deen Brothers' demolition techniques. In retrospect, hubris had caught the ageing leader in its grip as early as 1985. Seeking to emulate Margaret Thatcher, Bjelke-Petersen sought to break one of the state's most powerful unions, the Electrical Trades Union. Relying on his familiar tactic of declaring a state of emergency and pushing controversial and repressive legislation through parliament with little debate or forethought, the premier responded to a strike by SEQEB lines people by employing contractors.

When a picket line was set up, the striking workers were quickly dismissed and subjected to ever-greater individual penalties. Protest erupted, with remarkable scenes of priests and ministers carrying crosses and singing hymns being arrested becoming a commonplace. I remember seeing a woman with one leg, amputated at the hip, being bundled into a paddy wagon by burly cops at Victoria Park in Spring Hill. The power was out for much of the day, and support for the union was slim. Joh was again able to divide and conquer, and in 1986, when he claimed victory, the first election in which Nationals were able to form government without Liberal defections, he famously proclaimed that he had 'good news for Queensland – the lights will stay on'. Bizarrely, the Nationals' television ads during this campaign reminded citizens that Joh was like a father to them, that 'his love would never stop'. This interspersed with images of coalmining, naturally.

The rackets that interpenetrated the ranks of the police force and the parliament had become known as 'The Joke'. The joke ended up being on Joh, although the Premier was apparently lucky – his trial was aborted when the jury's foreperson, Luke Shaw, conveniently turned out to be a member of the Young Nationals. You could gain a sense of The Joke when Russ Hinze appeared on the telly, denying that there were any illegal casinos or brothels in the state, an assertion that any cab driver could have contradicted. The Police Commissioner, Sir Terrence Lewis, Hinze said, had taken him for a drive down Brunswick and Wickham streets in the Valley to show him exactly where each venue wasn't. The joke was on all of us, and we were all in The Joke. 'The Moonlight State' blasted this into oblivion, showing the coppers carefully supervising the movement of gambling tables from one side of Brunswick Street to the other, as the Bellino brothers had decided to open up more salubrious premises above a prominent nightclub rather than in back of a strip club.

Before these midnight moves were exposed to the light of day, it had been easy to go from the Gabba dogs across Stanley Street to the 'gambling joint' in full view of the Woolloongabba police station. A word to the armed bouncer would suffice, and you could enter a world where waitresses continually refilled pot glasses with scotch, sandwiches were served free, and your cab fare home arranged. I went there a couple of times with my boss, who was bounced one night by the cops for complaining that the blackjack game was rigged. He wasn't arrested, because he pointed out the absurdity of the police prosecutor having to explain his alleged public order offences took place in an illegal venue, but he was gone for the night. Another time, I was sitting next to a bloke in the real estate game who, unwisely I thought, told me he was the Liberal candidate for Chatsworth. It was said that Russ Hinze would come in after a flutter on the greyhounds and bet on credit, although I never saw him myself. Whether it was a mahjong game for money at a Chinese restaurant, protection rackets in the Valley enforced by a kung fu school, or unlicensed clubs that never closed, there was a plethora of underworld nightlife in Brisvegas, provided you opened your eyes and knew the right people. For people like my Grandma, God bless her soul, Joh was a kindly man, a good Christian, and Russ Hinze a strong force keeping Southern Sin away from Queensland, as she duly recorded a vote for the Nats each time a state election rolled round.

Joh's narrative was one of eternal progress. As the ads that showed Queensland a green beacon in a map of Australia turned red – Tasmania had floated off somewhere, and the rest of the state governments weren't all Labor, but I guess it was meant to suggest that Hawke and the socialists ruled all outside Sovereign Queensland – mentioned, everyone knew that he 'had made this state great'. In an age when politicians are tightly scripted, the Joh show appealed to some for its sheer audacity, its never-ending supply of colour and movement, and it's amazing to look back now at old video and see Joh and Russ and the gang slagging off at Quentin Dempster as a 'communist'. Life was supposed to be cheaper and simpler here in Queensland, and if there were fewer public services, so be it – to be a true Queenslander was to be enterprising and self-reliant. If you wanted to be looked after, you could always find a bloke who had a mate who knew a bloke. That was okay, that was natural 'free enterprise'.

This was all a joke because even us lefties laughed at it. And as Nationals periodically pointed out, the Labor party could never actually muster 50 per cent of the vote, or usually anything near it, so the gerrymander wasn't the thing keeping the Nats in power after all. Joh was Queensland.

JOH GOES TO DISNEYLAND

> Queensland is a state where chauvinism has been raised almost to a religion and where a divisive, confrontationist style of politics, coupled with a hugely unfair electoral system, has kept (Joh) in office when in other states premiers have come and gone. Queensland is more than a geographical entity. It is also a state of mind.
>
> Peter Charlton, *State of Mind: Why Queensland is Different*, 1987

Joh had been overseas at the time Bob Hawke called the 1987 election. He was in Disneyland as he watched his fantasy of 'going to Canberra' escaping his grasp. Cheered on by conservative commentators in *The Australian*, and financed by fast money from the Gold Coast white shoe brigade, his quixotic quest to rule the roost federally involved such improbabilities as Andrew Peacock serving as his Deputy Prime Minister. The only outcomes of all these shenanigans were the opening of a deep rift with the National Party machine led by Sir Robert Sparkes, and the crushing of John Howard's hopes of the prime ministership. But unlike Howard's Lazarus, Bjelke-Petersen was finished even though he didn't know it yet. Events could no longer be shrugged off with a casual, 'Don't you worry about that', and the premier's days in office were numbered.

Health Minister Mike Ahern was yapping at his heels, refusing to countenance the ban on condom vending machines the premier imposed, sending the cops to rip an offending machine out of the University of Queensland Student Union one night. Ahern stood for a modernised form of conservative rule anathema to the premier. Events moved on in such quick succession that Joh's house of cards came tumbling down all at once in December, when he first tried to sack most of the cabinet, a request refused by the governor, sacked five ministers, including Ahern, and then was sacked by his own party, but not before trying to stay in office with Labor's help. Peter Beattie later played himself in a dramatisation of these remarkable events at Joh's farm at Bethany, never one to avoid the cameras. Russ Hinze was reputedly reduced to shouting through the door of the Premier's office, 'Come out, Joh, it's over, mate', while the minister's massive frame shook with tears. The day that the seemingly eternal leader departed, I remember a huge storm brewing above Parliament House. The heavens mirrored the extraordinary events on the earth below.

5

REFORM FROM UNEXPECTED PLACES

Mike Ahern's regime, humane and principled in its support for democratic process and commitment to Fitzgerald Inquiry reforms, felt like an anti-climax. This was probably unfair to the new premier, but he had to make the best of it. In many ways, his modernising agenda was not too dissimilar to Labor's – the remnants of the Liberals tending to be more timid now – but introducing it from within the shell of the Joh regime was too hard an ask. It was easy for Labor to charge that the National Party could not distance itself from its dark past, particularly as revelations of evil and malfeasance continued to be reported from the proceedings of the Fitzgerald Inquiry almost daily. Ahern had deep roots in the Nationals, his father having been a Country Party president, and he had entered parliament young, in a by-election for Landsborough in 1968. But he was a very different style of politician: university educated – a rarity in a state where secondary education was rare enough, particularly for its aged country-born politicians.

Ahern was also a Catholic, and this was significant in a party whose sectarian hatreds had never been too far below the surface. The ebullient Archbishop of Brisbane, James Duhig, seemingly immortal and enjoying ecclesiastical office from 1905 until his death in 1965, had not been a confrontational figure like Melbourne's similarly long-lived Archbishop Daniel Mannix. As well as land grabbing, which saw many of Brisbane's heights occupied by Catholic churches, schools and convents, the jovial Archbishop sought to advance his largely Irish-descended flock through the ranks of the public service and professions. But people could still go to Toowoomba in the 1970s and see job vacancy signs in shop windows reading, 'No Irish Need Apply'. The Micks had colonised certain departments of state, most famously justice, but some power circles were closed to them. Catholic barristers tended to have a criminal practice, and many commercial chambers were Anglican and Presbyterian redoubts. Masons ruled the roost in the National Party, and Ahern was a lone duck before he became a lame duck premier.

Promoted by Joh on Russ Hinze's advice, more to head off a rival than recognise talent, Ahern had already proved his heterodoxy by chairing a committee that recommended sex education in schools, something anathema to Joh and later Education Minister Lin Powell, who was more inclined to want creationism taught. The former chief whip had taken on the redoubtable Rona Joyner, morals campaigner from Ipswich, and survived. As Industry Minister in the 1980s, Ahern saw early the possibilities of the digital economy, and foreshadowed Peter Beattie's 'Smart State' themes with an eye to a future not just about mining and farming. Ahern might aptly be described as a progressive conservative, and his inclinations on civil liberties and parliamentary accountability were not too distinct from those of the Liberal ginger group. He was not a man of reaction like Joh, always trying to hold back the tide.

The new premier, however, had little choice but to sit and watch as some of the ministers who had most strongly supported him, Brian Austin and Don Lane among them, joined Russ Hinze on what appeared then to be the road to jail. Hinze would never go to trial, dying of cancer before his case could be heard, but four National Party ministers and the Police Commissioner, Sir Terrence Lewis, all served time. Ahern could never square the circle, as the new ALP leader, solicitor and civil libertarian Wayne Goss, much more urbane and more probing in his parliamentary performance than his union official predecessors, put him under the spotlight at the same time as his own National Party administration plotted to replace him with the prisons' minister Russell Cooper, a grazier dubbed 'Joh's clone'. An attempt to extend the term of parliament, to deal with the Fitzgerald recommendations, failed, and Cooper, after an initial challenge ran Ahern close, took over for an ignominious administration of only six weeks.

Despite Cooper's warnings that gays would parade down Queen Street in the event of a Labor victory, on 2 December 1989 the electors finally ended the 32-year reign of the National Party, sweeping the remnants of the tattered regime aside against the gerrymander. Labor, in a campaign largely crafted by Wayne Swan, had road tested its approach with a 'three monkeys' mini-campaign, implying that Ahern sought to see no evil, hear no evil and speak no evil of his reactionary colleagues. It cut through because it was substantially true, and the Labor Party appealed for just one term to clean up Queensland, and duly received it from the electors. The last gasp of the old, the attempted revival of authoritarianism under Cooper – many Joh supporters saw Ahern as weak – ended with a whimper, and was seemingly expunged from the state's history.

GOSS REFORMS, BUT IS UNDONE BY KOALAS AND COPS

The pervasiveness of the dysfunction was not easily fixed. It was not just a matter of charging two hundred and fifty and finding more than half of them guilty including high profile police, businessmen and former government ministers, or passing legislation and implementing administrative reforms. Although the system was broken in countless ways it was also resilient. As those who challenged the status quo found at some personal cost, it would also fight to preserve the old ways of doing things in which everyone knew their place and rumour, innuendo and social networks were as influential as outright corruption and dishonesty.

> Julianne Schultz, 'Disruptive Influences',
> *Griffith Review*, August 2008

It was in the Beattie years that Labor came to be talked about as 'the natural party of government'. Wayne Goss' mission to bring about electoral and legislative reform had been a historic one, but it ended in disillusion, power slipping away amidst complaints about a new road infringing koala habitat. It was an inglorious end to a reign that began so promisingly, sweeping away the detritus of decades of conservative rule; a mere six or so years in office. Electoral boundaries were rendered fair, corruption cleaned out, and the public service modernised. Importantly, in a state where institutions and checks and balances were always weak, Goss echoed Ahern's promise to implement the Fitzgerald Inquiry's recommendations 'lock, stock and barrel'.

Among these recommendations were the establishment of independent commissions: the Criminal Justice Commission to fight organised crime and root out corruption, and the Electoral and Administrative Review Commission to recommend changes to electoral laws and bolster civil liberties. It was to Goss' credit that he was prepared to cede power to these bodies and allow them to frame the reform programme. This may be his most significant legacy as a reformer but it wasn't enough. The quotidian tasks of government sapped energies, the Cabinet was uneven in its quality, and those who'd looked to the ALP for the dawning of a new age of social liberalism were at best only partly satisfied. Wayne Goss, after stepping down as premier in the wake of the 1996 Mundingburra by-election, went back to university to complete an MBA. He was all set to take on Pauline Hanson in the 1998 federal election, but sadly the former premier suffered a brain cancer, a recurrence of which was to take his life, far too young at age 63, in 2014.

Goss' legacy, in pure political terms, was not a deep one. In a way, his regime had shallow roots in the Labor Party. Goss was more of the progressive-lawyer type, a civil libertarian, who in another state, perhaps, or had he come from a middle-class background, would have been odds-on to join the Liberals. Many of the significant figures of the Goss years were staffers and politicised public servants rather than ministers – something quite new in Queensland. One of the most famous, then and now, was Kevin Rudd. Oddly for a government that had made (probably too) much of sweeping out alleged National Party cronies from the public service, power centres revolved around Labor staffers and Labor-aligned political science academics who were key links in the command-and-control chain emanating from Goss' office in the Executive Building on George Street. Kevin Rudd famously sat in the office right next door, a literal gatekeeper. Both Rudd (nicknamed, unkindly, 'Doctor Death') and Peter Coaldrake, later to become Vice-Chancellor of QUT, were said to be unconcerned about summoning public servants for interrogation in the early hours of the morning. Ministers grumbled about staffers, foisted on them, who reported to the premier's office rather than to them. In many, many ways, the seeds of a future disaster for the sometime director-general of the Office of Cabinet and future prime minister were sewn in the Goss years. Many assumed that Rudd's public service background would have made him an efficient administrator. It was not so. Of the 'troika' of Goss, Rudd and Swan, who had steered Labor to a historic victory in 1989, only Swan really got the party's culture, although, intriguingly, he too had been a political science academic.

As *Griffith Review* editor and journalism academic Julianne Schultz relates in 'Disruptive Influences', reform wasn't as easy as the implementation of the Fitzgerald recommendations and the imposition of public service managerialism. The economic sands, and the landslide of the recession we had to have, shifted under the foundations of the Goss regime, and the shrinking of traditional agricultural and underground coalmining industries and the disappearance of the post offices, railway stations or sidings and bank branches that had been the hubs of many a small town and hamlet, saw a rather shambolic return to a Nationals-led Coalition Government in 1996, itself to collapse under the weight of One Nation in 1998.

By 1995, listening was not the Goss Government's strong suit. It wasn't just the koalas that brought him down, or the alleged complacency in the electorate about a protest vote (although that was also a factor), but the very command-and-control model that had been central to his success. A reserved man, Goss was not in the mould of 'strong' premiers past – at least not in his public presentation. Articulate, sharp and able to carry an argument forcefully, he nevertheless lacked the emotional connection with the people that previous leaders had, or represented themselves as having. On the Country Party side, Frank Nicklin had been an avuncular, almost a paternal figure, while Labor's Tom Burns was very much the knockabout larrikin, who named his tinnie 'the electorate' so his electoral staff could tell callers he was 'out and about in the electorate' with a straight face when he was in fact fishing, XXXX no doubt in hand. Too much had been assumed, too little spelt out, and public servants, their lives and routines shaken up by reorganisation and sometimes redundancies, vented their anger on Labor. Goss blamed Keating, but the fish and chips shop owner in Ipswich was no doubt pondering the decline of her own working-class mining town and the unfamiliar Vietnamese streetscapes of some of its suburbs while Paul was still riding high on the back of the true believers.

The Goss era had something of a flat feel; its early promise seeming fleeting. Some said that the arts lost their radical edge through recognition and government funding, and the hard hand of repression that had stimulated so much creativity had been lifted to no avail. Perhaps, but it's probably an unfair complaint. A lively band scene was to hit the Valley – now cleansed of its gambling joints if not its strip joints, and gay venues were out in the open – as retail businesses were sent to the wall as the recession reduced the price of rents. A generation younger than me, though, were sometimes heard to lament the excitement they'd missed with the disappearance of illegal venues. But not everything had changed.

I used to go to the karaoke night at Annerley's Chardon's Corner Hotel, in a suburb that was then quite rundown and very cheap to live in for students, and observed 14 year olds get served with a local copper sitting prominently at the bar chatting to the publican. When the clock struck ten, he'd say to Mick, 'Mate, I think your clock is wrong', and the publican would literally turn it back. Licensing laws had yet to be overhauled – absurdities persisted such as the necessity for band venues like the Zoo and the Sitting Duck to offer patrons plates of cauliflower because it was impossible to get a liquor licence without selling food – and pubs still closed at a dismal 10 pm. The Joke had not entirely departed the scene, if you knew where to look, and Wayne Goss' tetchiness when confronted with continued evidence of police misbehaviour, particularly against Indigenous people, might have indicated a certain frustration that the past could not, after all, be banished by legislative fiat.

The Goss Government didn't fall all at once. It was brought down eventually by a by-election in the marginal Townsville seat of Mundingburra, which was strictly speaking a re-election as the original result had been declared void by the Court of Disputed Returns. The winner, a Liberal, was the former cabinet-maker Frank Tanti, not a candidate renowned for his deep thoughts on policy, and in a way a precursor of some of the interesting characters who were to be swept into parliament just two years later as One Nation members.

REACTION REACTS BADLY

Goss walked, rather than face a vote of no confidence in parliament, and Rob Borbidge became Queensland's first post-Fitzgerald National premier, leading a minority government supported by Gladstone independent Liz Cunningham. Borbidge had been a junior minister under Mike Ahern, rising to Police Minister in the brief Russell Cooper Government. A Victorian immigrant, drawn to the Gold Coast by Joh's abolition of death duties, the member for Surfers Paradise was an urban National, and therefore, a rare bird. His brief premiership, in double harness with the

Liberal leader Joan Sheldon as Treasurer and Deputy Premier, was riven by scandals surrounding a memorandum of understanding with the Police Union, an organisation made notorious in the Joh era. The union was given power of veto over senior appointments, allegedly in return for political support and a donation towards the by-election campaign.

This affair haunted the Premier, and shenanigans around an inquiry into the matter by the CJC were superseded by an enquiry into the CJC itself, which promptly led to the resignation of the original judge. Yet another enquiry, in true old Queensland style, exonerated everyone. But this was hardly a good look, and nor was the setting of mounted police on revellers at a 4ZZZ market day in Musgrave Park, a decision former Premier and Police Minister Russell Cooper failed to defend cogently or even coherently. 'Don't you worry about that' was not really good enough in 1997, and Borbidge also faced the revolt of his own bush base over John Howard's acquiescence in Wik Native Title legislation and, even worse for the farmers, the gun legislation that followed Port Arthur.

Pauline Hanson had already been elected to federal parliament, of course, the fish and chips shop owner having been disendorsed by the Liberals before the 1996 federal election due to her racist remarks. Both the state Coalition and the federal governments now had to face a real threat to their right, but many Labor voters in Queensland were also attracted to Hanson's style and rhetoric. The perception that Paul Keating had governed for 'elites' and minorities had taken hold, and equally as important, the losers from his political and economic projects did not intend to take defeat lying down. Hanson swept 11 MPs into office in the state election in 1998, a campaign dominated increasingly by the National Party's overruling of Premier Borbidge's injunction to put One Nation last.

Labor and Nationals both lost seats to the colourful insurgents, including a fisherman and a department store Santa, but Labor won more, and was able to govern initially with the support of Nicklin independent MP Peter Wellington. Wellington was to support Labor again into minority government in 2015, and insisted on transparency and community participation as a condition of his support on both occasions. Beattie responded by instituting 'Community Cabinets', where the ministry would meet openly, often in a suburban or regional area, and meet with the community and take questions. As with a number of Beattie's innovations, this was subsequently adopted by Prime Minister Kevin Rudd in the federal sphere. Later, a by-election, caused by the resignation of a One Nation member in Mulgrave, enabled the Beattie-led ALP to govern in its own right. Meanwhile, the motley crew of One Nation MPs fractured every which way, some forming a 'City-Country Alliance', some sticking with the party and some becoming independents. The latter was the best path to political longevity, with Dorothy

Pratt holding Joh's former seat of Barambah until 2012.

Some compared the One Nation members to the first Labor MPs in the 1880s and the 1890s, unschooled representatives of the people. But the big difference was that the first Labor members were often autodidacts and, more crucially, had a strong sense of common purpose and a social base. In any event, the last One Nation representative, Rosa Lee Long, was finally defeated in 2009. Strangely, Long's late husband had been of Chinese descent, an oddity for a party with its first plank being a revival of the White Australia cry, directed at Asian immigrants, in an echo of some of the 'anti-Chinese' riots that plagued Queensland in the 19th century. In any case, One Nation was a considerable shock to the political system.

The 1998 election was effectively a four-party race, with Liberals rushing to support Borbidge and distancing themselves from their alleged rural Coalition partners, and the insurgents came second, outpolling both Liberal and National party voters that were considered separately. In seats out west where properties were large, and traditions of deference to the grazier class well entrenched, the Nats weren't massively troubled, but in areas of closer settlement, they were run close or smashed. Similarly, the fringes of Brisbane to the north and Logan and Ipswich to the south and southwest elected One Nation MPs in place of Labor members, or turned electorates into contests between those two parties, with the Coalition reduced to irrelevance.

REFORM FROM UNEXPECTED PLACES

Whether or not the Nationals learnt much is questionable – particularly since Bob Katter, who had left the party federally in 1993 and who had been a Joh acolyte and a minister at a young age during his career as a state member, was to revive much of One Nation's economic populism and agrarian socialism in 2012, with considerable success. Peter Beattie, though, was quick to see that the path to modernity was paved with potholes, and act accordingly.

SWIMMING WITH SHARKS

Everything Prime Minister Kevin Rudd knows about anti-political politics, the politics of the larger-than-life charismatic leader throwing a spanner in the works of the political machine, he learnt from Beattie. So there's a certain pleasing symmetry in PB joining up to Team Rudd, the 'media tart' who first invented 'Team Beattie' as an alternative brand label to the miniscule 'Queensland Labor' (and thanks to the National Archive for preserving the web evidence).

Beattie learnt his politics in the leafy groves of Brisbane's western suburbs, part of an insurgency that was one of the afterlives of the concentration of anti-Joh energy that radiated outwards from the University of Queensland's sandstone cloisters in the 1970s. Long before he was state secretary, his method was to run against his own party, which with some distinguished exceptions like Senator George Georges, looked a lot like the Left wing of the corrupt Joh 'joke'.

As premier, Beattie took populism to a fine art. Affable and composed, he presided over a regime that had its fair share of failures (and it's been somewhat graceless of him to criticise Anna Bligh, given that some of those failures were visited on her). But he courted popularity by always being ready to apologise for the failings of his own government, and switch tack with alarming rapidity.

> Mark Bahnisch, 'Peter Beattie is the Anti-Politician Rudd and Labor Need', *Crikey*, 9 August 2013

Peter Beattie, a colourful character if there ever was one, was in my estimation the best politician (at least at state level) Australia has seen in the last few decades. An energetic man, the young Beattie was the driving force behind the party's upheavals in the late 1970s, a prime mover behind the first meeting of the ALP Reform Group in a hall in leafy Bardon. Academics, teachers, lawyers and professionals joined a very small group of progressive unionists to demand change in how the Labor Party oligarchy did its business. The Breakfast Creek old guard responded by denouncing the middle-class insurgency as, well, 'academics', a swear word it would seem. Of particular horror was the involvement of 'radical feminists' as well as that of Senator George Georges, a courageous leading light in the civil liberties movement, whom the old guard wanted to expel. With the antediluvian and anti-abortionist Ed Casey uneasily straddling the perilous heights of the parliamentary party leadership, the moustached young Beattie provided a contrast in his frequent TV appearances. Some things never change.

After stoushes galore, court cases, and federal intervention driven partly by federal leader Bill Hayden – an Ipswich boy who must have been tearing his hair out at the shenanigans in his own back yard as he prepared to challenge Malcolm Fraser for the prime ministership – UQ historian Denis Murphy emerged as president and Peter Beattie as secretary. But memories were long, and the dissolution of the old guard hegemony brought factionalisation in its wake, as well as the opportunity for Joh to utter one of his more favourite bon mots, a variation on his standby, 'the left wing, the right wing and the chicken wing': 'the old guard, the new guard, and the mudguard'. Nobody knew what Joh meant, except that disunity was said to be death, and the new guard fractured between the centre (actually the right and dominated by the re-affiliated AWU), the centre left and the socialist left. Peter Beattie, perched on a slender limb with the small centre left, consisting largely of branch members and with only slight union support, ended up as a member of the old guard, now rebranded as Labor

Unity, a faction whose members would insist, over interminable post-Labour Day beers at the International Hotel in Spring Hill, was 'the real left', whatever that signified.

Fast forward a few decades and Peter Beattie turned minority government and electoral scandal into a Labor landslide in 2001, after symbolically going swimming in a shark pool before the campaign. Beattie's genius was to reconcile the old and new Queenslands, pursuing a research-, technology- and creativity-led industry strategy at the same time as cosying up to Joh and wowing the backwaters of the state with his folksy style, and opening up cabinet and parliamentary processes to the community. Beattie, after all, was a child from the bush, a native son of Atherton, far to the north on the Tablelands, and he never neglected to make much of this. Privatisation was resisted; padding in the Queensland Rail workforce defended, because livelihoods depended on it, and transitions should be slow; and populist impulses like indefinite detention of paedophiles who had served their time acceded to. When Beattie did social liberalism, it was usually by sleight of hand, with little trumpeting. Thus the lessons of One Nation were learnt, and the Premier, like Joh before him, but unlike either Borbidge or Goss, began to blend into Queensland itself. Paradoxically, though, Beattie, a former chair of the Parliamentary Criminal Justice Committee, presided over a government perhaps less than saintly on probity issues, as Tony Fitzgerald has subsequently argued, and ministerial scandals, and even blatant corruption and malfeasance in the repulsive incarnation of Minister Gordon Nuttall, were tolerated for far too long.

It was always a puzzle to observers as to whether Beattie was sincere, particularly in his regular backflips, executed with consummate ease, and always after a 'listening tour'. Most spectacular was his quick move to surgically excise offending MPs and party officials after the revelations of the 2001 Shepherdson inquiry into electoral corruption, not least his own Deputy Premier Jim Elder and prominent AWU figure Mike Kaiser. Beattie made a few personal selections for vacant seats, and won a massive landslide on the back of the inquiry, winning 66 out of 89 seats and reducing the Liberals to a shadow party of three. Beattie had no love for the AWU, of course, and it was its propensity to tolerate or even encourage not just branch stacking but false enrolments that had landed him in what should have been political oblivion, but which he turned into political triumph.

The truth is that Beattie is a big personality, and one who loves interacting with people. Some friends of mine saw the premier in a penguin suit outside the convention centre one time, where a punk concert coincided with a mining industry dinner in an adjacent hall. They yelled down for a lift back to Wilston, the suburb both they and Beattie lived in, and Premier Pete obliged. Such stories are legion, and travelled quickly in a town like Brisbane, still made up of small and interlocking circles despite its pretensions under Campbell Newman to be a 'New World City'. So Beattie was both ebullient and calculating and, like many a priest, had a phenomenal memory for names and faces – quite a contrast to the personally reserved Goss. He also had the good judgment to depart at the right time, having groomed Treasurer Anna Bligh as his successor.

BLIGH SAVES THE STATE, BUT NOT THE PARTY

Anna Bligh featured prominently alongside Peter Beattie in election posters and billboards in the 2006 election. Bligh, MP for South Brisbane since 1995, when she replaced Minister and socialist-left luminary Anne Warner in the West End-based electorate, was another product of the campus activism at the University of Queensland in the late 1970s and early 1980s, when struggles around land rights and against the repressive laws introduced by Russ Hinze coinciding with the Commonwealth Games were at their height. Politicised early, a Catholic schoolgirl from the Gold Coast who had once considered becoming a nun, became a feminist activist, social worker and public servant. Bligh, the first woman to be elected premier in her own right in Australia, saw her somewhat more sophisticated style come undone after a narrow victory in 2009, with a backflip on privatisation – always hated in a sprawling and decentralised state – costing her legitimacy, despite her sterling leadership during the disastrous floods of 2011.

Bligh had seemed to inch away from Beattie's interventionist industry policy, abolishing the Department of State Development and pursuing a more conventional fiscal line. Her authority questioned by some of the male dinosaurs still lumbering around in the party, she responded by accepting too much advice from political strategists, trying to project 'strength' by wearing hard hats in photo ops and grabs for the nightly TV news. Perhaps this was a response to fears about being the first female premier the state had seen, although the volume of misogyny directed at Julia Gillard did not appear to be replicated locally. She was always at her best in unscripted interviews, warm and intelligent, but it wasn't until the end of the 2009 campaign that she threw out the rulebook, strongly challenged the legitimacy of ratings agencies to dictate austerity policies during the global financial crisis. This was so inconsistent with the sharply announced privatisations, perhaps masterminded by Treasury and enthusiastically embraced by young Treasurer Andrew Fraser, that a deficit of trust opened up much bigger than the fiscal deficit she was seeking to address.

Superb in her command of detail, a quality much on display during the Brisbane 2011 floods, and a fine contrast with the somewhat erratic performances of Campbell Newman, who at one stage wanted the military to blow up a floating riverwalk, her stubbornness became her Achilles heel. This was a pity, as her awe-inspiring calm, command and emotion during far too frequent disasters displayed her leadership qualities in spades, and she continues to occupy a place in the hearts of many Queenslanders. I had friends in Sydney who watched, horrified, at the coverage of the Queensland floods as they devastated the Lockyer Valley and then Brisbane. It was impossible to maintain much composure living through the deluge, as even if you were safely high up above sea level, you worried terribly about friends and fellow citizens in the path of the rampaging river. My flatmate and I had relocated from the partially flooded New Farm, although we were above the flood line, fleeing the absence of electricity to my dad's place in Ashgrove. Brisbane, or at least the unflooded bits, had become an eerie place, with no cars on the roads and sometimes a shortage of food in the shops. We eventually decided to turn off the 24-hour TV coverage, which was just proving too upsetting.

It's to the eternal discredit of the Murdoch press that it indulged itself in one of its absurd campaigns, seeking to lay blame for the force of the flood on either engineers or the Queensland Government, or both. A Royal Commission in 2012 found almost everything was done by the book, but the shameful attempt to lay the blame for an extreme weather event at the feet of politicians and public servants was a disgrace. The problem lay in the book itself, written during the 1980s and prioritising the river crossings beloved of farmers near Lowood over the release of water

REFORM FROM UNEXPECTED PLACES

that might have saved Brisbane, a tale of Queensland parochialism writ small. Bligh came into her own during the floods, communicating superbly, as well as showing genuine feeling and empathy. The flood was a most disturbing event, and we were lucky that the waters receded when they did, as you could almost feel the social fabric fraying as Brisbane began to fear being cut off from food supplies. This was the state at its best, fulfilling its basic responsibility to keep its citizens safe, but going the extra mile at that.

Bligh was probably unfortunate to have inherited the premiership at the end of a long Labor incumbency. Many problems had simply compounded, with the bloated and incompetent bureaucracy of Queensland Health for instance becoming such a running sore that the Premier, in my view, made a very sound choice when she promised to abolish the organisation. Wherever you go in Queensland you can see spanking new modern hospitals, but Labor receives little credit for these, nor do they for the creation of public transport and bicycling infrastructure. The public was in a tetchy mood, and the media uniformly hostile. Bligh, a former Education Minister, left a legacy in this portfolio that will endure, successfully introducing prep and bringing Queensland into line with other states, which had long had 13 years of schooling. The state also experimented with specialised selective high schools in aviation, creative arts and maths and sciences, seeking to lay the path for the industries of the future. It might have been less spectacular than Peter Beattie's Smart State numberplates, but it was possibly a more significant change than many aspects of his industry policy. The Premier did herself no favours through a refusal to change course on privatisation, something her predecessor was famous for, and the Labor Party did itself no favours through a failure to renew the ministry, many of whom were by this stage of the game either tired out or talentless time servers whose chief attainment was an iron grip on office. In a way, 2009 was the election Labor should have lost, but Anna Bligh can always be proud that she was Premier at the right time, the time that she was needed most.

Finally, privatisation was always a step too far for state Labor, and the bizarre spectacle of 'Strong Choices' ads in the 2015 campaign showed that the LNP recognised its unpopularity. This far-flung state always relied on public infrastructure and spending, whether its aim was developmental or ameliorative. The generation of Anna Bligh and former Treasurer Andrew Fraser followed the logic of state finances that had become the boilerplate of fiscal wisdom across the eastern seaboard, and crashed and burned in its wake. The ironic outcome of the Labor modernisation project was the forgetting of Queensland's difference, and an assumption that the public would cop the logic of Treasury finance and merchant banking, an assumption that cruelled Bligh's term almost before it had begun. Retribution was terrible come election night.

6

ENTER BOB KATTER, THE GHOST AT THE FEAST

As his ever-patient assistant chief of staff flitted in and out, reminding him of a radio interview he had scheduled, he relaxed and his answers became less evasive. By the time he left to go on air, I was still wondering whether the Katter presented to the public was real. But delving further into his book, I became less sceptical. Katter takes seriously those topics that had bored me when I studied Australian history at school. It is a book of heroes in the story of Australia's development. Those he reveres include Edward 'Red Ted' Theodore, a socialist and financial genius who became the federal treasurer during the Great Depression; coal titans such as Les Thiess; Country Party leader John McEwen, who pushed for tariffs and protection for the manufacturing industry; and the postwar prime minister, Ben Chifley, who increased immigration and kick-started the Snowy Mountains Scheme. Katter regards history as being dictated not so much by grand ideological movements as by the character or lack of character of the men involved. His giants pushed ahead with their grandiose schemes even when everyone doubted them. Seeing them through Katter's eyes, I realised I had always taken their significance in the development of the nation for granted.

> Louis Nowra, 'The Heart and Mind of Bob Katter', *The Monthly*, April 2013

Queensland election night, 24 March 2012, is etched in my memory. I'd spent an unpleasant afternoon handing out how-to-vote cards for Grace Grace, the member for Brisbane Central, at the Merthyr Uniting Church booth just a street away from my apartment in inner-city New Farm. I was on the booth with federal Labor Senator Claire Moore, a mate, and we felt as if we were being subjected to a continual onslaught from uncharacteristically uncivil and angry voters, one of whom screwed up an ALP how-to-vote and threw it in Claire's face. This wasn't enjoyable, and the only good vibes we were getting were from gay men, always strong supporters of the party that had liberated them from the closet. If it was like this in the inner city, we wondered, what was it like elsewhere? It boded very badly for the Labor faithful.

That night, I was at a party in Stones Corner, on the fringes of then Premier Anna Bligh's seat of South Brisbane. The day had been punishingly hot, and there was little relief from the heat. A very improvised gathering – snacks hurriedly purchased at the 7-Eleven and grog from the Brunswick Hotel bottlo – it was not a night of good feelings or merriment. I remember resolutely staying outside to avoid the TV coverage. I vividly recall reassuring one non-reveller that there was little to be gained, and everything to be lost, from watching Antony Green and Kerry O'Brien recite yet another Labor seat falling to the LNP. It was not a happy night for Labor and Greens supporters in South Brisbane.

During the campaign, I'd been working on a project initiated in partnership with *Crikey*'s then editor, Sophie Black, researching the impact of coal seam gas development, particularly on the rich farmlands of the Darling Downs. An exercise in mixing social science research techniques and public interest journalism, our bet had been that we could make a difference by highlighting and communicating intelligibly a complex issue the major parties were largely agreed on. As it turned out, perhaps precisely because of that bipartisanship, but also because for different reasons The Greens and Katter's Australia Party failed to gain momentum, CSG only simmered rather than burnt as an election issue. But I did spend an afternoon drinking in the Jondaryan Hotel with young KAP candidates.

QUEENSLAND

Sheltering in the ramshackle timber and tin structure from 39-degree heat outside, we conducted a remarkably interesting political conversation, the Akubra-topped participants and observers shooting the non-existent breeze over schooners of XXXX. Hence, on election night, I was summoned indoors from my perch on a log, where a local's guitar gently wept, to watch and listen to Bob Katter on the telly. I can't remember his exact words, but The Man in the Big White Hat rained on Campbell Newman's parade. These days, the Kennedy MP warned, Newman and the LNP could just as easily find themselves on the opposite end of the drubbing Queenslanders had just given to Anna Bligh and Labor. And that could happen in 2015.

Although Queensland has a history of occasional lopsided election results, the dimension of the LNP's victory in March 2012 was unprecedented. After a six-week campaign interrupted by a federal Labor leadership contest between Kevin Rudd and Julia Gillard and rocked by the failure of Premier Anna Bligh to substantiate allegations of corruption against LNP leader Campbell Newman, the ALP plummeted from a governing majority to just seven out of 89 seats in the Legislative Assembly. The victorious LNP won 78 seats on the back of a swing of 15.2 per cent. Labor, as we've seen, had been in power since 1998, initially as a minority government under Peter Beattie, but then enjoying successive landslide victories in 2001 and 2004 and a comfortable win in 2006. The first female premier of Queensland had led the party to a 'come from behind' position in 2009 to secure a fifth term. No doubt longevity in office was a prime mover in Labor's 2012 defeat. Important also was the amalgamation of the Liberal and National parties, eliminating disunity and division on the right of state politics. The particularities of Queensland's electoral system and voting culture, with optional preferential voting and a propensity to 'just vote one' for the elector's party of choice, also facilitates lopsided and disproportionate distributions of seats. However, the sheer scale of Labor's defeat still requires explanation.

While a number of states, most spectacularly Victoria under the Kennett Government, and federal governments of both political stripes had long adopted policies in public management and the privatisation of assets and services squarely within orthodox neoliberal parameters, Queensland had, once again, been different. Historically a low-tax jurisdiction, its public services were underfunded compared to the national average. The Beattie governments sought to increase funding, particularly to health and education, while at the same time pursue developmental industry policies designed to reorient the state's economy away from a disproportionate reliance on agriculture and mining. Concurrently, the sheer distances within Queensland and its relative decentralisation increased the costs of providing high-quality services. Beattie did not wish to depart from the fiscal orthodoxy of surpluses and low taxes. During the boom of the 2000s, the circle could be squared, but the impact of the GFC brought a quick and disturbing end to a seemingly virtuous circle of low taxes and high public spending. Something had to give.

Anna Bligh won in 2009 by standing up to global finance and ratings agencies, vowing to fight to keep jobs in Queensland. But only a short time after Labor's re-election, a sweeping programme of privatisation, most significantly of Queensland Rail's freight business, was announced with little attempt to set the scene. Ostensibly, the sale of state assets would restore the state to fiscal health, although this was rightfully disputed by impartial analysts. Labor's trade union and electoral base fractured almost instantly, and while Premier Bligh gained kudos for her leadership during the disastrous 2011 Queensland floods, the trust deficit massively outweighed the alleged fiscal deficit. The LNP opposition was also gifted a campaign theme of 'Labor's debt and deficit', as the ALP had legitimised this narrative through its justification of the privatisations.

AUSTERITY COMES TO TOWN

As later with the election of the federal Coalition Government in 2013, this theme justified the quick abandonment of the rather moderate and anodyne election promises made by the LNP in opposition ('more jobs, better services'). Predictably, a Commission of Audit, headed by former federal

ENTER BOB KATTER, THE GHOST AT THE FEAST

Treasurer Peter Costello, reported that the state's finances were in worse shape than anticipated, paving the way for unflagged austerity measures, the most controversial and obvious of which was the dismissal of a large number of public servants. The claims in the report were at best dubious and at worst pure rhetoric. Crucially though, the report foreshadowed a very limited role for the state – restricting the functions it manages and administers rather than competitively funding the basics: the courts and police. Everything else was potentially up for grabs, subjected to tendering by the private sector.

Such nostrums are often dismissed as pure ideology, or as a wish list. However, that is to mistake the purpose of these documents. Reports like Costello's are not akin to an electoral manifesto or a programmatic plan for public sector management. No one should anticipate their early, or indeed full, implementation. Rather they represent a coherent vision of the world as it should be, one dominated by the supposed superiority of competition and private interest over state provision and the public interest. Just as the drumbeat of calls for 'greater productivity' through individual contracts and the diminution or elimination of union power that are repeated in countless statements by business groups, leaders and the financial press do not represent an evidence-based assessment of actual barriers to productivity, so too the Costello Report is disconnected from the immediate situation, pointing instead to a desired future. Hence, the 'rubbery figures' and the dominance of assertion over evidence.

Campbell Newman's government, enjoying an unprecedented parliamentary majority, might have been expected to take a leaf out of New South Wales Liberal Premier Barry O'Farrell's book and proceed slowly but resolutely. The genial BOF was well aware that his party held huge swathes of natural Labor territory, and was determined neither to frighten those horses, nor to succumb to the temptation of acclaim by the right-wing media for introducing radical 'reform' that had not been foreshadowed to the people in the campaign. Newman's approach couldn't have been more different. It was as if a blitzkrieg was being executed. The keys to the Executive Building were grabbed the day after the election, the Labor Party consigned to the wilderness through its symbolic chucking out from Parliament House, and a massive solar project near Chinchilla cancelled and the Queensland Premier's Literary Awards abolished in short order. Public servants were sacked in droves, and the Premier took to breaking promises with abandon, alarming his own followers by comments like his assertion that he was disposing of Labor's mess with his 'pooper scooper'. The nasty insinuation about Anna Bligh was no coincidence. Sometimes locals claimed that the Premier had had one too many whiskies (Newman in a flattering profile for the *Courier-Mail*, written by a sports journo, had admitted this was his nightly tipple) when the House was sitting late at night, such was the vitriol that escaped his lips. Rather than the adult government Queenslanders had been promised, what we saw was the launch of a seemingly never-ending series of wars on everyone and everything, from the poor old flying foxes to respected professions such as medicine and law.

Queensland can, of course, be prone to lopsided election results. Witness the two Peter Beattie landslides in 2001 and 2004, and Joh Bjelke-Petersen's demolition of Labor in 1974. If we go back to 1996 and 1998, though, we can perceive another pattern that's looking increasingly prevalent nationally and internationally (just ask anyone in the United Kingdom): victories that are anything but knife-edge majorities and hung parliaments. The consummate politician of his era, as I've argued, Beattie played minority government for all it was worth. But the meltdown of the Coalition Government in 1998 over the issue of One Nation preferences, and the subsequent electoral showing of One Nation – outpolling both Nationals and Liberals counted separately, and the election of 11 MPs – was a pointer not just to the need for Nats and Libs to unite but also to much, much more. The Palmer United Party, the Liberal Democratic Party, the Democratic Labor Party, Katter's Australian Party, country independents, Shooters and Fishers, on and on and on, were elected seemingly ad infinitum. The electoral system in the federal House of Representatives discourages all but rural independents, but a significant number of voters persists, across the gamut of contests they asked to adjudicate on, in casting their votes for populist or splinter parties of the right with a frequency that should now suggest this is the new normal rather than an aberration.

As we've seen, some of the most colourful characters of the populist push, of course, are Queenslanders, starting with Joh and his quixotic campaign for Canberra in 1986 and 1987. Traditionally, and this is true for the distinctive Queensland Nationals style of politics and politician too, this variety of personality-centred populism had decreasing electoral returns the further south of the Tweed you go along the east coast. That still holds true, I think. PUP at its height was a largely Queensland-based phenomenon, or so the polls told us. But most would struggle to name any of the new Victorian right-wing upper house MPs and, Nick Xenophon and David Leyonhjelm aside, few of the federal senate crossbenchers who aren't PUPs or ex-PUPs could be described as charismatic. Think John Madigan, although he's impressed me in interviews, so I'm not making a pejorative point here. The argument is, however, that, aside from the well-known sociological reasons that underpin eccentric politics in the Sunshine State we've already reviewed, something broader is going on across the nation as right-wing parties struggle to contain an increasingly free-floating discontented vote. Remember, like Campbell Newman, the former Coalition Government in

ENTER BOB KATTER, THE GHOST AT THE FEAST

Victoria and Tony Abbott federally won mainly through being 'not Labor'.

NEWMAN OVERREACHES AND VLAD LOOMS LARGE

In 2012, it would have been difficult to accuse the Queensland LNP of being policy free, if you restricted yourself to tallying up the number of documents posted on its website. Once, though, you discounted such gems as 'legalise the playing of two-up on Anzac Day', most of them boiled down to a familiar diet of slogans: 'More Jobs, Better Services'. Newman, leading the party from outside parliament, had been a relatively non-political leader at the time, his image shaped by his 'can do' style in Brisbane City Hall. The Mr Hyde to Can Do's Dr Jekyll was the combative and thin-skinned figure who was to become only too familiar to Queenslanders until his reincarnation as a Zen message machine in 2014. The Premier, as part of 'Operation Boring', tried to talk more calmly while repeating the message of the day over and over again. Still, the LNP won largely on the grounds that it was competent and 'adult', that it would be a 'no surprises' administration, and that it would fix the mistakes Labor had made. Holding an electoral coalition together in government, and governing cohesively and in the public interest rather than throwing raw steak to the dogs of the 'base' and the conservatariat, though, that's a different thing.

Queensland, it's often claimed, is a naturally conservative state. I'm not sure what to make of this claim, at least at the level of electoral and party politics, when we consider that the state was the first to elect a Labor Government anywhere in the world, that it saw the first general strike anywhere in the world in 1912, that it had (albeit decreasingly radical) Labor governments from 1915 with only one interruption until 1957, and then again from 1989 with only one interregnum until 2012. Queensland elected the nation's only Communist Party MP, Fred Paterson, Member for Bowen, in 1944.

You could argue the converse, of course, on the basis of the Joh hegemony and Queensland's distaste for federal Labor, but the point is that this doesn't prove the state is a conservative bastion in the face of Labor's record at state level for much of the last century. And, as Carole Ferrier and Raymond Evans argue cogently in *Radical Brisbane*, the traces of a radical history have already been necessarily erased, both geographically and from the textbooks and the received narratives. The fact that civil war almost broke out next to the government printery in George Street during the conscription referendum in 1916, as a clash between Queensland police and armed supporters of Billy Hughes was narrowly averted, rarely features in the canon of Australian history. Evans takes university students and others on walks around radical Brisbane, and much of the time he has to conjure up an image as the reality has long disappeared, except when the Commissariat Stores on William Street are visited. One of Brisbane's oldest structures, built by convict labour, the Royal Queensland Historical Society presents a very sanitised version of the convict period, and the stones are made to say something other than the awful aura embodied in them during the building's construction.

Campbell Newman won in 2012 not by projecting an ideological face or by appealing to some supposed innate conservatism of the electorate but through the exact opposite. Yet he led a government that seemed obsessed with humiliating enemies, with starting fights, with indulging itself in flights of fancy like removing the requirement for water fluoridation and dressing imprisoned bikies in pink jumpsuits. The government disdained both evidence and consultation as it careered from crisis to crisis, and absurdity to absurdity. Unemployment surged, jobs disappeared, and the economy tasted increasingly sour.

Overkill was a big part of the Newman years. The notorious VLAD laws – Vicious Lawless Association Disbandment, more popularly known as the bikie laws – rushed through parliament after a shooting was followed in short order by a violent public brawl on the Gold Coast, threatened to strip electricians of their licences, imprisoned a female library worker for having a few of beers at the pub with a couple of mates, and segued into the attack on the judiciary. Magistrates had a pesky habit of granting accused people bail, despite the imprecations and dire warnings uttered by the boy wonder of the Newman Government, Attorney-General Jarrod Bleijie. To his eternal credit, Independent MP for Nicklin Peter Wellington hammered the government on the excesses of this legislation up hill and down dale as the Labor Party equivocated. Suddenly, the newly appointed Chief Magistrate Tim Carmody took into his own hands all bail hearings by alleged bikies. Carmody was elevated in quick succession to the Chief Justiceship vacated by the respected Paul De Jersey, anointed Governor. Newman, who insisted that Carmody's appointment was his call, appeared to be trying to send a signal to the judiciary that they had to be in closer lockstep with the government, particularly around sentencing.

Newman admired Carmody's working-class origins and his background as a policeman. What Newman didn't mention was that one of the new Chief Justice's judgments had been overturned on appeal during his previous service on the Family Court, and that he has been found to have 'cut and pasted' parts of the judgment from a case with different facts. Carmody was also the head of the LNP's inquiry into child protection, and had found that the Wayne Goss cabinet had been wrong to shred documents related to the 'Heiner affair', a convoluted scandal from the late 1980s that provided much fodder for the more conspiratorial fringes of the right. Carmody also recommended putting children from 'dysfunctional families' up for adoption, and reinstituting institutionalisation for teenage delinquents. Whatever the merits of Carmody's work on children in care, these were themes likely to appeal to the Premier, whose youth justice policy had been to dismantle restorative justice programmes in favour of boot camps.

Thus a war broke out with the judiciary. Solicitor-General Walter Sobronoff QC resigned and blasted the government and the Attorney-General in the press. Bleijie was accused of leaking a conversation he had with the President of the Court of Appeal, Justice Margaret McMurdo, herself the occupier of a position once held by Tony Fitzgerald. All hell then broke loose, with Peter Davis, the President of the Bar Association, resigning in protest, and a very public boycott of Carmody's ceremonial installation by his fellow justices.

WAR IS DECLARED ON DOCTORS

If this wasn't bad enough for the government, a war on the doctors was being fought simultaneously. Queensland Health and its administration, or rather maladministration, had been a continual irritant for the Bligh Government, contributing mightily to its downfall with revelations that a 'fake Tahitian prince' had embezzled millions while billions were thrown at IBM to try to recover a payroll system that failed to pay people correctly or on time. However, the public trusted the hospital system to a degree that might surprise, given the scandals surrounding surgeon Jayant Patel, called 'Doctor Death' by colleagues. Peter Beattie had concluded an agreement with the salaried doctors in 2005, raising wages and attracting talented doctors from other states and overseas, as well as retaining many Queensland-trained medicos in the hospitals. Newman's managerialism and LNP ideology combined to make a toxic blend: an insistence that all doctors sign individual contracts and placing pennies before patients under the rule of Ian Maynard, Newman's hand-picked director-general, an associate from his council days. As often as the Premier and Health Minister Lawrence Springborg could rant about 'interstate union thugs' and demonise individual doctors under parliamentary privilege, the 'Keep Our Doctors' campaign had a counter: the phenomenal energy that hospital doctors put themselves into contacting their fellow citizens.

Unable to demonise bikies successfully, the Newman Government was on the way to a hiding in seeking to paint judges and surgeons as agents of chaos or subversion. It was incredible, and the government paid heavy electoral prices in by-elections in Redcliffe and Stafford, the latter won by maxillofacial surgeon Dr Anthony Lynham for Labor. The Stafford by-election was caused by the resignation of sacked Assistant Health Minister, Dr Chris Davis, himself a well-respected former president of the AMA. Davis had come close to openly siding against his own government at one of the doctors' Pineapple Meetings, mass gatherings at the

ENTER BOB KATTER, THE GHOST AT THE FEAST

Pineapple Hotel in Kangaroo Point, speaking courageously just after the tragic and untimely death of his daughter. But that was not the issue he chose to resign on; it was the government's emasculation of the Crime and Misconduct Commission, successor to the CJC and Queensland's version of New South Wales' ICAC.

The Newman Government, displeased by the investigation into its handpicked CMC Acting Chair, Dr Ken Levy, had spectacularly sacked the entire parliamentary committee charged with the body's supervision, chaired by long-term independent Liz Cunningham. Opposition to further changes had been one issue behind Davis' sacking by Newman, and the changes to electoral donation laws, effectively enabling the LNP to escape accountability for many of them, was the last straw for the MP. Having subsequently announced his intention to join the Labor Party, Davis resurfaced during the 2015 campaign in a series of powerful print and television advertisements attacking his former party on integrity issues, in one of which he described the LNP leadership as 'sociopaths'.

The War on the Doctors was said by LNP sympathisers to be 'strategic' instead of just 'tactical' (that was apparently the War on the Lawyers and Courts). They seemed to be saying that the Newman Government needed to demonise its public health workforce in order to achieve its obsessional goal of switching public employees onto contracts, and to prepare the ground for mass outsourcing and privatisation in the health domain. Observers, and for that matter campaigners, were often puzzled by the moves made by the Queensland Government in the campaign. While some facets of its approach to health and public sector employment relations made sense – for instance, the appointment of Ian Maynard as Director-General of Health was widely interpreted as being about driving a whole of government efficiency agenda in one of the state's largest areas of expenditure and employment – others seemed inexplicable. The government at times seemed to be determined to undermine shaky trust further by virulent attacks on highly respected individuals such as Nobel Prize winner Professor John Fraser, was seen to have concocted an auditor-general's report to justify its campaign, and struggled to argue a cogent case for either the necessity or desirability of the contracts.

Rational political observers felt that it would be in Newman's and the government's interest to intervene to settle the dispute (and indeed the Parliamentary Labor Party repeatedly called for such an intervention) but the Premier instead publicly announced his intention to recruit interstate and overseas doctors, and his disinterest in the threatened resignation en masse of doctors who had given long and altruistic service to the Queensland public hospital system. Most of the time, in its public rhetoric, the government appeared to inflame the dispute and demonise its 'enemies' rather than seek good faith resolution in a calm fashion. How can all this apparent madness be explained?

Again, as with the landslide defeat of Anna Bligh and Labor, there are factors that are relatively clear. For example, the Liberal and National parties are far from united despite their formal amalgamation, and the LNP is factionalised both within its parliamentary party room and between its parliamentary leadership and the organisational wing. There were multiple tensions around leadership and jockeying for influence in Cabinet. The conservative parties had been in opposition since 1998, and had only enjoyed a brief and shambolic period in government from 1996 to 1998, effectively an interlude in a very long period of Labor rule from 1989, itself ushered in by a collapse in the standing and coherence of the Bjelke-Petersen and subsequent National governments. The National and Liberal parliamentary parties had been devastated numerically in 2001 and 2004. So, in terms of political experience, there was little around. Lawrence Springborg, the Health Minister, was only briefly a junior minister in the Borbidge Government and, surprisingly for a relatively young man, was the longest-serving MP and 'Father of the House'. But most of his service had been in opposition, having been elected in the 1989 poll that swept the late Wayne Goss to power despite the feared gerrymander. Hence, no doubt, the selection of a proven figure in Campbell Newman (bizarrely, but significantly without a parliamentary seat) as leader, and the subsequent recruitment of a number of senior officials and business advisors who had worked for the Brisbane City Council or advised Newman as mayor. Hence, also, the emphasis on the role of local government and on decentralisation, in any case a favourite theme of the rural and regionally based Nationals.

JARROD BLEIJIE PROMOTES HIS YOUTUBE CHANNEL

Similarly, the combative nature of the government can be explained not just through the personalities at its centre, but also through the 'thinness' of its win despite its numerical predominance, and the lack of policy development and cultivation of cooperative relationships with key corporate and community actors during its long spell in the wilderness. Remember Bob Katter had popped up on election night warning Campbell Newman that the tide that had swept him so spectacularly to power could recede just as quickly. But this was not the view of the LNP, busy building itself a new Tower of Mordor, a $2 billion office building on William Street, which would house the government right next to a casino, presumed to be operated by James Packer. Backbenchers, many of whom had not expected to be elected, were spear carriers for the Cabinet rather than representatives of their constituents. They were quickly under pressure from constituents, shocked by the mass sackings, and could tell which way the wind was blowing, and didn't like it one iota. Some busied themselves with mad campaigns, such as body-builder Member for Nundah on Brisbane's northside, Jason Woodforth, who warned of the evil consequences of fluoridation in drinking water. Even though former leader John-Paul Langbroek, a dentist, said this was crazy, the government was quick to give local councils the ability to 'opt out' of fluoridation. This was not what electors had envisaged.

Likewise, the extraordinary weakness of checks and balances in Queensland's unicameral parliament exacerbated a tendency to hair-trigger reactions and the introduction and passage of ill thought-out legislation with little consultation or scrutiny. Parliament was witness to bizarre speeches from Attorney-General Jarrod Bleijie, raving about his YouTube channel and karaoke skills, when it was meant to be debating the emasculation of the Industrial Relations Commission and the removal of public servants' permanency of employment.

Some of these factors were shaped by the personalities and the politics of the day, and others were more long term. But missing from a standard political science explanation is the particular content of the public sector contracts, whether for doctors or for the rank-and-file administrative staff in departments, now devalued as not being 'frontline', and the relevant legislation. It's here that attention given to the apparent truisms enunciated in reports such as Peter Costello's is crucial – claims that the private sector is always more efficient, that individuals should take prime responsibility for their own life outcomes, that unions are malevolent bodies interposed between cooperative staff and management, that deficits are evil, and so on.

All this highly contestable and often untrue discourse translates into political common sense, and leads directly to the sorts of long-term fractures in the equitable funding of public health traced above. It provides a 'common sense' menu of measures for conservative (and far too often, Labor) politicians from which to choose on any given occasion or in any particular policy and political conjuncture. At the same time it both creates and empowers private corporations that seek to cherry-pick the 'profitable' parts of the range of services provided in health and other sectors, and fund conservative parties and right-wing think tanks, and health economists who are happy to operate on the terrain of assertion rather than evidence-based policy. It's precisely this too often unexamined consensus in favour of the private and against the public that needs confrontation. It didn't escape the attention of the union movement or of the new Labor think tank, the TJ Ryan Foundation, and rallies soon became a regular feature across the state, organised around the protection of the public sphere, no matter how absurd and ridiculous the government's various distractions and outbursts became.

As it turned out, Bob Katter was right. The LNP's public support disappeared as if in a flash. Labor won back power in one term. What accounts for such an astonishing train of events, an electoral cataclysm that sent the country's right-wing newspapers into meltdown, stentoriously warning that the nation was now doomed, ungovernable in the face of public resistance to reform? The answers lie in Queensland's history, political and cultural.

As we've seen, in the 1970s and 1980s, claims that Queensland was different from the rest of Australia abounded. Over the not quite three years of Campbell Newman's premiership, interstate observers might have been forgiven for assuming that Anna Bligh had been a temporary modernising blip on the storm radar, and that the Sunshine State had reverted to type. Whether seeming eccentricities like declaring war on bats or allowing councils to opt out of water fluoridation, or the more serious and even spectacular wars on not just bikies but also doctors and the judiciary, a lot of envelopes were being pushed that would remain sealed in other states. The brown paper envelopes stuffed with hundred-dollar notes were a thing of the past, but it appeared to many that the spectre of Joh Bjelke-Petersen had not just been evoked, but had risen from his Bethany grave. Defence lawyers were branded as conspirators, the environment scorned and trashed, development lauded to the skies, and dissenting voices treated as enemies to be silenced. Respected clinicians were vilified in parliament during the virulent doctors dispute, the independence of courts and arbitrators stripped away by rushed legislation, and consultation openly dismissed as futile. All this needs to be read in context with the continuing attack on and devaluation of public servants and the very concept of serving the public, and the contempt for the rule of law and for any opposition to the numerous 'Strong Plans' enunciated from on high. The irascible Premier, prone to hyperbole in his parliamentary performances, as we've seen, had claimed that he was taking out his pooper scooper to 'clean up Anna Bligh's mess' – code, it seemed, for sacking public servants en masse. School nurses went by the wayside, patients were told to bring their own towels and pyjamas to hospitals, essential medical clinics were scrapped, waiting lists were wished away by the creation of a 'waiting list to get onto the waiting list'. The 'Great God of Surplus' gobbled up much that was good, offered up as a living sacrifice of people's livelihoods and sense of security. And respected figures, including Tony Fitzgerald, almost a Queensland saint in the public mind for his service and his integrity, trashed by the thuggish Deputy Premier Jeff Seeney, were constantly berated, attacked and denigrated. The switch to Operation Boring, and the mindless recitation of the adjective 'strong' could not wipe clear the slate, and the memories persisted up to election day. Queenslanders prided themselves on having banished the hungry ghosts of the state's dark past, and as Brisbane writer Andrew Stafford has observed, the desire to get off the Joh merry-go-round again was palpable.

7

CAMPBELL GOES EARLY

"In my view, the LNP's most colossal misjudgement was that the Queensland electorate – particularly those in the urban enclaves of greater Brisbane which hold so many of the state's seats – somehow still pined for the days when Joh Bjelke-Petersen ruled the state with jack boots and an iron fist. (Actually, perhaps the first thing the party executive should do is sack whoever advised the LNP to get the word "strong" into every utterance, from every pulpit and press release, as often as possible.)

Large segments of the LNP still haven't accepted history's verdict on the Joh years. The gavel came down hard with Tony Fitzgerald QC's report in 1989, which banished the conservatives from office for a generation, barring a Bob Borbidge blip in the mid-1990s. Newman, the former Brisbane Lord Mayor, was recruited as a putative premier from outside the parliament to put an acceptably urbane face on the newly merged Liberal and National Parties. Once elected, though – with a monumental majority that saw the

> ALP reduced to a rump – it took about five minutes for the "Here we Joh again" comparisons to start flying.
>
> Andrew Stafford, 'Why Queensland Will Never Joh Again', *Friction*, 2015

Campbell Newman must have seen his doom written in the stars, because he called an unprecedented January election – the first on mainland Australia, as psephologist William Bowe noted, to be held in that month – just after the New Year fireworks for 2015 had been launched. I was in Surat Thani, a bustling industrial and port city in Thailand, and I was in Singapore when I wrote my first column for *The Monthly* on the campaign. It wasn't just I who had been caught on the hop. Newman had clearly wanted to catch the opposition unawares, and had hoped that Queenslanders would have forgotten the spectacle of a barnacle-encrusted federal ship of state sinking into Christmas oblivion.

Operation Boring, on the advice of conservative pollsters and strategists, would give way to 'Operation Repetition'. The 'Premier was Strong', his 'Team was Strong', and only the LNP had a 'Strong Plan for Queensland', a bag of goodies for each electorate premised on the 'Strong Choice' of asset sales. Semantically odd, these mantras were nevertheless to be repeated at every opportunity, and presumably drummed into the minds of voters, to result in an LNP victory on 31 January, just after kids had gone back to school and the year was gearing up for business. Certainty would prevail.

Any rumour retailed by Clive Palmer loses credibility just by virtue of its messenger. But the small world of Brisbane had been awakened from its post-G20 holiday slumber by tales that the LNP, not the most united of strong teams, was about to jettison its leader. Campbell Newman is said now to have a literary future, and maybe his memoirs will recount what was in his mind as he saddled up to face the music, but we may remain as ignorant as the several senior ministers who were relaxing on holidays on Sunday when the Premier's office leaked the news of the impending campaign to the *Courier-Mail*, increasingly seen as the LNP's mouthpiece since a recent change in its editorship. What we can infer is that far from the orderly progress towards a triumphant second term, the Queensland conservatives feared defeat. The hope seemed to be that no one much would think too deeply about anything over summer, and that the rebadging of asset sales as 'leases' would smooth over the bitter medicine of privatisation. Voters were to think only of the good things they would get once the assets were sold.

QUEENSLAND

NOT SO STRONG CHOICES

The campaign, however, refused to follow the script. Enter Alan Jones, the conservative shock jock whose opposition to coalmining and the destruction wrought on the town of Acland, where he was born and now literally removed from the map, portended ill for Newman. Jones relocated to Brisbane and spent an hour on the radio each morning damning the LNP and Campbell personally with well-targeted jeremiads. Only one week in, reeling like a man on the ropes, Queensland Premier Campbell Newman denounced the Labor Party for Alan Jones' accusations of bad faith. Newman was stuck in a groove, perhaps still smarting from Anna Bligh's accusations about his family finances and lord mayoral reign in the 2012 state election campaign. Newman sought to quash the sometime friendly fire from conservatives by suing Jones for defamation, a tactic that smacks of desperation. It was also a tactic beloved of Joh Bjelke-Petersen, whose litany of defamation actions against opposition members was legendary, and fully funded by the Queensland taxpayer – Newman stated, in response to questioning from Opposition Leader Annastacia Palaszczuk, that the LNP was funding the action he and Deputy Premier Jeff Seeney brought against the veteran shock jock over his allegations about the Acland Mine.

Newman and the LNP were copping more flak from traditional allies than from Labor. Maybe this partly explained the low-key vibe of the LNP launch, although the incongruity of surrounding the Premier with both Jeff Seeney and hijab-wearing family members of Yeerongpilly candidate Leila Akubar, a former refugee, did not go unnoticed, just as the spectre of the absent Tony Abbott attracted a Bill Shorten zinger or two. The first week began with two policy launches – Newman's being characteristic of the Operation Boring that had been underway since the disastrous Stafford by-election to stem the government's sagging election fortunes. The premier promised, as was now his wont, all manner of good things – provided voters swallow the bitter pill of privatisation. Youngsters were to get teaching scholarships (well, some of them) and free drivers' licences (if they behaved). Probably key to the Premier's appeal, though, was his plea to 'just vote one'. The Premier lived in fear of a hung parliament. Maybe Tony Abbott's on-again off-again GP co-payment didn't help much.

Meanwhile, up in Coolum, state PUP leader John Bjelke-Petersen revived memories of his dad by promising to eliminate payroll tax altogether. Bjelke-Petersen implied that Newman had betrayed the Joh legacy. Queensland was no longer the low-tax destination for southerners and foreign capital, although – again bizarrely – the Premier echoed the late Sir Joh by declaring Queensland 'sovereign' when asked if Prime Minister Tony Abbott would be joining him on the campaign trail. Palmer was absent from his own launch, apparently confined to bed with a touch of the flu. Amidst bells and whistles lacking from the major party launch, JB-P, who looks a lot like his dad, and has run unsuccessfully for parliament thrice before, for the Nats, LNP and then PUP in the federal election, promised the abolition of payroll tax, support for solar energy, and an international airport for Maroochydore. Curious that the forces of populism – in this case, although not in all, reflecting the people – wanted to talk up renewable energy. But Bjelke-Petersen's platform was probably a tad moot. What was important was that PUP and KAP were not preferencing the LNP, and were providing alternatives to the government from the populist right.

So to Ipswich, traditional heartland for both Labor and Pauline Hanson (who stood under the One Nation banner just up the road in Lockyer, and came within a whisker of winning), where Labor leader Annastacia Palaszczuk launched her campaign, after countering the LNP and media rhetoric about its absence of a fiscal strategy with just that the Friday before. Palaszczuk spent the weekend decrying asset sales, and not promising, while Newman continued to hold out billions to the voters, only if they supported the said asset sales. Labor was trying to restore its tarnished reputation as economic managers, pledging to pay down debt with income from state enterprises, and contrasting its modest measures with the LNP's spendathon. Whether there would have been any shekels left to put towards the promised land of the AAA credit rating by the end of the campaign must be considered doubtful. The rate things were going, it would all go on roads to everywhere and nowhere, which along with coalmines and casinos, was seemingly the centrepiece of the LNP's job-creation efforts.

By contrast, Palaszczuk presented a well thought-out package of measures to both stimulate job creation through innovation and research and skill up jobseekers through employment programmes and the revival of TAFE. Despite a *Courier-Mail* splash, Anna Bligh wasn't there at the Ipswich launch although Peter Beattie, who confusingly said he wouldn't be because he was now a political commentator, was. The party faithful, as with the LNP troops, dressed in civvies rather than campaign shirts, were receptive to a measured and calm presentation, which hit all the right notes, particularly in its peroration – a plea to voters who might have been thinking again of voting Labor to look to policy rather than the past. Palaszczuk, although not always completely assured in her media efforts, provided a pleasant contrast to the combative Premier by radiating calm and humility.

A reminder of the reason why Newman was there in the first place, his reputation as a socially liberal Brisbane Mayor who could get things done, also surfaced as a video was uploaded showing Campbell touting the virtues of solar energy and pointing out, reasonably, that Queensland couldn't always rely on coal. With the other pillars of the economy he had promised to nurture collapsing, Newman in office appeared captive to non-renewable resource interests. The LNP rode high on donations from coalminers, and promised to splash cash at any coalmine they might wish to develop, even if it was commercially dubious. Captured by the active forces of the religious right within the LNP, the then candidate for Ashgrove, despite his proclaimed support for same-sex marriage, had spent the 2012 campaign equivocating over the Labor Government's civil unions legislation. Paradoxical? Not in the light of the history of parties of the right in the Sunshine State we've already perused. Campbell Newman had tried to straddle too many fences, and some of those were decidedly rickety, held together with fishing wire in the wake of the Labor victories that had prompted the formation of the LNP in 2008.

Unsurprisingly, in the face of Peter Beattie's then dominance, both Nationals and Liberals were plagued by leadership tensions. The 'NSW disease' of revolving-door leaders was actually a Queensland disorder before it ever infected politics south of the Tweed. With the exception of the brief and unlamented Borbidge/Sheldon Coalition Government, destroyed by One Nation in 1998, the conservatives were usually up the creek without a paddle, although the Nationals' ship was steadied by 'The Borg'. Lawrence Springborg had contested two elections unsuccessfully before a final try as inaugural leader of the LNP. His big idea – an amalgamation of the two conservative parties – successfully garnered in most of the anti-Labor votes, remnants of One Nation notwithstanding. By 2008, when the Liberal National Party was formed, the small l liberals were but a memory, and it was up to once and future federal MP Mal Brough to try to save a separate Liberal Party.

Springborg, a rather quaint figure famed for growing enormous pumpkins, warning of the dangers of 'feminisation' apparently inherent in recycled water and for being photographed ironing in a singlet, failed to straddle the city/country divide. Brisbane voters, long neglected by the fly-in fly-out graziers who were born to rule and saw George Street as just a theatre of political grandstanding and a conduit for patronage and pork-barrelling, needed one of their own to wean them from Labor. Enter, not without controversy, Campbell Newman. Brisbane lord mayors, administrators of budgets not so far short of Tasmania's, had long been towering figures. Whether it was Clem Jones who sewered the city and built the freeways, Sallyanne Atkinson who ushered in Expo '88 or Jim Soorley who revived the inner city and graced the river with CityCat ferries, mayors of both parties had made a difference. While Newman's concrete achievements, it was often said, were limited to seemingly endless tunnels no one drove through, his 'can do' image and social liberalism were just the trick for detaching Brisbane voters from an uncertain Labor faith.

Cursed to live in interesting times, a fractious backbench in a bloated parliamentary party came back to haunt

Newman. In truth, whatever the Premier's intentions, power was wielded largely by the party administration, a very country affair, and his back watched by Deputy Premier Jeff Seeney, described by one of his own Nationals colleagues as 'the most hated man in the bush'. Whether it was the youthful zeal of Attorney-General Jarrod Bleijie (an invisible man in the campaign), the lure of PUP and KAP for disillusioned backbenchers, the necessity of keeping the religious right in the sheepfold, or just the governing traditions of the Queensland right ('development', 'private enterprise', 'strong leadership'), Newman reverted to type, inscribing himself into the mould of premiers past. If the LNP actually was improving frontline services, no one would have noticed, so belligerent was the government's image. Toned down after the disastrous Stafford by-election, Operation Boring ended during the campaign with allegations of cronyism and lying around Great King Coal dominating the airwaves. That Newman resorted to the Bjelke-Petersen tactic of trying to silence dissent through a lawsuit suggests that Campbell was a prisoner of the past, not just of whatever transpired between him and Alan Jones (a topic on which I think it's wise to make no comment), but also on the colourful and tawdry traditions of the right in the Sovereign Sunshine State.

PRINCE SIR PHILIP, WHILE NEWMAN STAYS 'STRONG'

Fast forward to the Australia Day weekend, and the Newman train had run off the rails altogether. Desperate times make for desperate measures, and the measure of Campbell Newman the man was front and centre in the Queensland State Election campaign in its final week. Having accused Labor of receiving bikie money funnelled through unions in the People's Forum at the end of the penultimate week of campaigning, the Premier's gambit when asked to provide evidence was to say, 'Google it'. LNP ads went into overdrive, but all anyone with thumb on mobile could find when the dust settled were some opportunistic and ironic donations from bikies to the LNP, and a fleeting edit to Newman's Wikipedia page suggesting he had organised crime links. By Australia Day, the Premier was determined to be back on message, a message that might have been lost in the static as electors pondered whether Prince Sir Philip, just given a gong by Tony Abbott, might now have his own little corner of Queensland, befitting a beknighted consort. By Tuesday, Newman was expressing his view that Tony Abbott's 'knightmare' had been unwise, but on Australia Day itself Campbell answered every question put to him by journalists by reciting his nostrums about 'strong plans', a 'strong team' and 'strong jobs'. He explained that he was answering questions ordinary Queenslanders wanted answered.

Whether or not electors were interested in 'strong plans' was unclear to most at this stage. It was certain, though, that the LNP was not having a good week. Labor released its 'modest' costings, but by Thursday, when the Premier had flown back from north Queensland in an unannounced and some said panicked change to schedule, no one was much concerned at his and the Treasurer's response. Rather, the man standing next to him, Tim Nicholls MP, Member for Clayfield and Treasurer of Queensland, the same man whose election signs in his blue ribbon seat no longer bore the LNP logo, had suddenly come into sharp focus as a possible premier. *Seven News* had released a ReachTEL poll showing Newman behind Labor in his own seat of Ashgrove, 54 to 46. The margin was almost identical to Newman's lead at a comparable stage of the 2012 race, but this time the late surge had been towards Labor's Kate Jones, seeking to regain the marginal seat she had held from 2006, until the Anna Bligh wipeout. Constitutional lawyers opined on whether the premier had to sit in parliament, an ironic echo of Newman's own path to power as an opposition leader without a seat. Suddenly, the ruling party's claim that a vote for anyone else would lead to chaos seemed ironic too. Labor had become the party of stability, and the spectacle of either a quick by-election or an unseemly scrabble for the vacant premier's chair loomed large.

Labor, meanwhile, was playing it safe. Days went past without a policy announcement, as the party and its leader Annastacia Palaszczuk rammed home the message that an ALP Government would not sell state assets. The ALP's 'modest' costings were contained in a document of modest length, and the party's law and order policy consisted largely of a commitment to consult on a review of the notorious bikie laws. The champion of the rule of law, Tony Fitzgerald QC, gave a very rare interview to the ABC's *7.30 Report*, decrying both parties and complaining of a creeping culture of corruption sneaking back in ever since the Goss Government. Fitzgerald advised his fellow citizens to vote for neither major party.

THE ELECTION RESULT NOT PORTENDED IN THE SKY

Queenslanders duly went to the polls on 31 January 2015, a sweltering day across the length and breadth of Queensland, from Currumbin to Cook. As the day dawned, federal Libs were scrambling to talk about 'natural corrections' and the 'cost of hard decisions'. 'Strong choices' weren't mentioned, despite the endless mantras from Campbell Newman during the election campaign – 'a strong team' with a 'strong plan'. Nor was the human cost of so-called reform, all the lives upturned through unemployment and the shrinking of opportunity that comes not just from public service cuts but also from the ultimate logic of austerity politics – the withdrawal of the state from actively supporting communities

QUEENSLAND

and individuals in their basic struggles. No, that was not it, just swings and roundabouts. Probably the LNP did not see the swing coming, could not quite believe that having surfed into a position of unprecedented dominance in 2012, holding 78 out of 89 seats, that the tide would turn. In any event, the LNP high command had reconciled itself, maybe not so unhappily, to the captain going down, but not the ship.

Expectations were uniformly for an LNP victory with around 50 seats, although Ashgrove would not be among them. Early on Saturday night, a row of largely middle-aged and completely white men in grey suits on *Sky News*, before a vote had been counted, made outcome predictions that represented an intriguing level of consensus. It didn't matter whether it was Graham Richardson, David Speers or Craig Emerson – the LNP was going to win about 50 seats, Labor about 35, and Campbell Newman would probably be defeated. I can't say whether or not any mea culpas were chanted later in the evening as I promptly switched channels to the Antony Green show on the ABC. As we found out pretty quickly, it looked very probable indeed that Labor would either win the unwinnable election or just fall short, but nevertheless be in a position to form government, and that the Premier would indeed be on the wrong end of the Strong Choice made by the good burghers of Ashgrove. Citizen journalist Margo Kingston, economist and commentator John Quiggin and I had been saying, as early as the Australia Day holiday, that it was quite possible Labor would win. Yet most accounts of the actual result were prefaced by the claim that 'almost no one had seen the result coming'. This seemingly unforeseeable seismic event then sent shockwaves across the nation, precipitating a farcical leadership coup and counter coup in the Northern Territory Country Liberal Party, and quickening the pace of Tony Abbott's implosion as federal Liberal leader.

As anyone would have told the *Sky News* crew, and perhaps as a few had said themselves, this was Queensland, and anything could happen. And it did. Newman's other mantra – that if he didn't win Ashgrove, the LNP wouldn't win government – was suddenly looking like coming true, but in a way that constituted his worst nightmare. This election result was about much more than swings and roundabouts, and about much more than the fate of Campbell Newman himself, now in the history books as a premier who lost his own seat. The pork-barrel truck was running on empty, it would seem, and Campbell will now have to formulate his own personal strong plan for his own future, post-politics. The reasons for Campbell's political demise have been analysed often enough, including by me in these pages, and no doubt the analysis is not at an end. With Newman's political career in the coffin, the ghost of National Party premiers past ought also to be interred.

If the voice of Queenslanders said anything on election day in early 2015, it thundered a rejection of the culture of power unrestrained and politicians crazed with hubris and arrogance. No more bills passed in the night stripping citizens and workers of fundamental rights, no more dodgy donations, no more jobs for the boys and girls, no more 'don't you worry about that'. Queenslanders decidedly voted in massive numbers for a return to accountability and the basics of good government and democratic practice, conventions trampled so far underfoot by the RM Williams boots of the LNP ministers over the past term. Any Queensland government will need, from now on, to understand that there can be no going back to the dark days of the past, that there is no electoral reward to be had from 'strong plans' that don't factor in the human cost of unrestrained crony capitalism, no electoral reward from 'strength' if that means treating citizens with disdain and contempt.

Let all the misgovernment and malfeasance come to an end, and let it be unmourned. There was a sly charm in the old Queensland, a seductive whisper that the state's distinctiveness was expressed through its baroque tropical politics, a humour beneath the cattleman's hats. But Russ Hinze is dead, he's not sleeping; he was never a King or an Emperor, even if Sir Joh was a knight, and after this year's state election, he should never be coming back. Lawrence Springborg and the LNP – take note. And Tony Fitzgerald QC should have rested more comfortably in his bed as the state inched towards the formation of a Labor government, albeit relying on the vote of independent Peter

Wellington, in an uncanny echo of the formation of the Beattie minority government in 1998. Wellington made explicit his support for transparency and accountability in an exchange of letters with Annastacia Palaszczuk, and indicated that she and he shared many of the same concerns. Hopefully Fitzgerald takes heart from the hordes of ordinary Queenslanders who, although voting against the ramshackle regime of the LNP for many reasons, will no doubt have been influenced by the sheer audacity of the joke that Campbell Newman's crew tried to play on what should be a modern and democratic state. Even on polling day there were appalling reports flooding Twitter of voters being denied declaration votes due to identification restrictions, and the LNP headed to the Supreme Court (unsuccessfully) to silence dissent by complaining about GetUp! how-to-votes and Labor signs.

POWER MOVES BACK TO THE PEOPLE

The party whose signs were subject to an election-day injunction is Labor brought back from the dead. While it's absolutely legitimate to criticise the ALP campaign, distorting the scale of its comeback by talking about 'natural corrections' is rubbish. If we go back in time to a comparable wipeout, Joh Bjelke-Petersen's reduction of the opposition to an 11-person 'cricket team' in the 1974 election – when Labor leader Percy Tucker, compared unfavourably at the time by Mungo MacCallum to a lettuce leaf, lost his own seat – the 'natural correction' in 1977 was a small one, and it took Labor until 1983 to regain most of the seats it had lost to the Coalition. Labor has now re-grasped power after just one truncated term.

Politics does move much quicker these days, of course, but the decimation of the Parliamentary Labor Party in Queensland in 2012 was a unique event in electoral history. Reeling under the blow, the party was in chaotic disarray, signified by Central Ward in the ensuing Brisbane City Council elections having three Labor candidates in one day – the first candidate stepped down for health reasons; defeated state MP Grace Grace sought to shift spheres but was stymied by electoral law; and, finally, Peter Beattie's wife Heather was drafted. After having promised to govern with grace and dignity, the new Premier evidently forgot magnanimity and kicked the miniscule opposition out of Parliament House, relegating them to a public service building in Margaret Street, a few blocks away. The seven remaining MPs from a pre-election caucus of 51 regrouped and elected Annastacia Palaszczuk as leader. Swings against Labor in seats they had held had been as high as 21.3 per cent. Now they have swung back in the opposite direction, often by the same order of magnitude. Having made history in 2012, the Queensland voting public has pulled off the same trick in 2015.

Palaszczuk, a lawyer by training and an MA graduate of

the London School of Economics, had followed her father Henry, a veteran MP and popular Minister for Primary Industries into parliament in the safe seat of Inala in 2006. I'd known Annastacia well at university, and was fond of the occasional political chat with Henry when opportunity presented itself. A good listener, and very responsive to community voices, the novice parliamentarian rose quickly from parliamentary secretary through a junior ministry to Transport Minister. It's unlikely, though, that Palaszczuk had been carrying a leader's baton in her backpack, and she certainly wasn't mentioned in dispatches as a future leader. Anna Bligh, it was assumed, would anoint youthful Treasurer Andrew Fraser, and Education Minister Cameron Dick was talked about as a potential rival. Both lost their seats to the LNP in 2012.

It is absolutely to Palaszczuk's credit that she grew in stature over the last term, and to the credit of the seven MPs (whose number grew to nine after a couple of stunning by-election wins in 2014) that they were able to provide a viable opposition but also to come tantalisingly close to victory so soon after Labor's Armageddon, and finally form a minority government. This was achieved not just through parliamentary efforts, but also through returning the party to its bases in the labour movement and the community.

As with the Victorian election, journalists were inclined to miss the enormous grass-roots effort – volunteers, thousands of phone calls and door knocks and, more importantly, a politics of community consultation. Labor's 'modest' policies had not been plucked out of a political strategist's hat, but rather emerged from intensive listening to many impacted upon by Newman austerity politics – whether nurses and ambos or bus drivers and Indigenous people. Labor also recruited an astonishingly diverse array of candidates, notwithstanding the six defeated MPs who re-contested and took back their seats this election. Among these candidates, many elected to the Legislative Assembly, are Leanne Enoch, the state's first Indigenous woman MP and now a minister, as well as electricians, defence lawyers, medical specialists and tradies – so much for the claim that the major parties always draw only on the political class. It's these connections with professions and trades, and the deep links made by Labor MPs into the manifold and multifarious communities that make up a diverse state, that have ensured not just its survival, but also a resilience that positions the party not just for an astonishing victory but also very well for the future.

The election is a vindication of the sense that so many have of Queensland as a project, a work in progress, but progress to a more humane, more inclusive, more transparent, fairer and more accountable polity and society. That project, the legacy not just of figures such as Tony Fitzgerald and the late Wayne Goss but also of a multitude of activists and citizens over the decades, has shown its strength when tested against the flimflam of 'strong plans' offered by a rattled party in a state of advanced decay. Political nostrums that have endured for ages should be tossed out along with the many, many LNP MPs who have lost their seats. And Labor, although it will tread softly, has learned the key lessons of its defeat in 2012 – that privatisation is poison, that Queenslanders want a government that respects not hectors them, and that there's life still in social-democratic politics, provided it connects with citizens.

The election result was truly an astonishing one, and its implications manifold. The political rulebook was smashed to smithereens along with the LNP's majority, and every political party must now take stock and listen to voters. The LNP, though, didn't accept its defeat well, or indeed at all for a couple of weeks after election night.

THE BORG VERSUS PREMIER PALASZCZUK

Oh my God. I've only just realised. Lawrence Springborg and John-Paul Langbroek are two different people.

I don't know how this happened. Nobody told me. I mean, I suppose I wasn't paying attention. Whenever some long, dark-haired streak of misery loomed out of the telly on behalf of the gubbermint, I knew it wasn't the short-arsed shaven-headed bloke in charge so it had to be Lawrence-Paul Springbroek. Or John Hyphen Langborg.

QUEENSLAND

> You know, the tall one, who was that one they had when Can-Do was still just Lord Mayor. Before Can-Do put on the I'm With Stupid T-shirt and surrounded himself with so many duds and plonkers that wherever he turned that T-shirt could not tell a lie.
>
> John Birmingham, 'Will Spring-John Broekborg be Premier?', *Brisbane Times*, January 2015

Why the apocalyptic rumblings dubbed #blamethevoters on Twitter, and how could a Murdoch columnist seriously propose 'the suspension of democracy', what anyone else might reasonably call fascism? How did the Queensland result send shockwaves that rocked the conservatives all around the nation, precipitating a farcical coup and counter-coup in the Northern Territory CLP, and the rapid meltdown of the captain whose pick of Sir Duke Prince Phillip had also helped blow any residual hope the LNP might have had out of the water on Australia Day weekend, 2015? How could the Queensland LNP get it so wrong subsequently, clinging desperately to office, electing Lawrence 'The Borg' Springborg – who had already lost three elections to Labor – in an attempt to woo two Katter's Australian Party MPs for support, even though the numbers just weren't there?

Evidently, the event that was the election was not over on the night of the 31st. All eyes might have turned to #libspill, the meltdown of Tony Abbott's leadership and the Queensland result itself, but Queenslanders, of course, continued to observe the bizarre spectacle of the Liberal National Party in deep denial. First, the diminished party room, at the apparent instigation of the last Country Party machine in town, the LNP party organisation, recycled two failed leaders, Lawrence 'The Borg' Springborg and John-Paul Langbroek, with the apparent purpose in mind of negotiating – despite there being no arithmetical path to an LNP majority – for government with two Katter MPs who despised the rest of the party's senior members. Confused mutterings in the *Courier-Mail* suggested that the faction of denial had prevailed against the reality-based community at the LNP's three-hour meeting, that those who had wanted to accept the result – of a democratic election – had been outvoted.

In the days following, it became almost impossible to avoid the droning voice of The Borg explaining that somehow he should be commissioned as 'caretaker' premier, and continue to administer if not govern the state until some hypothetical by-election, prompted by the ineligibility of a PUP candidate to stand for the seat of Ferny Grove, won by Labor's Mark Furner. Conveniently, because any sitting of the Legislative Assembly would have an ALP majority, with the support of Nicklin-independent Peter Wellington, parliament would not sit during this time. Captivated by the spectacle, the ABC's *State Bulletin* featured live interviews with both Lawrence Springborg and the state's last National

Party premier, Rob Borbidge. The balance police must have been off duty. It took a few days for the media to notice that there were people who actually knew about things like constitutional law and political conventions, and that one of those people, University of Queensland Law Professor Graeme Orr, was describing the LNP's bizarre machinations as an attempted 'constitutional coup'.

For this unlikely sequence of events, it's possible to look up the political playbook and find an explanation to hand: 'the LNP is trying to create an aura of illegitimacy around an incoming Labor minority government'. Maybe so, but that might be to ascribe too much political rationality to Lawrence and his crew. It's also plausible to suggest that they're enacting what they had warned against – the 'chaos and uncertainty' or a 'hung parliament' and that they, just like *Sky News*, had no ability to foresee an eventuality that would see them out of office. It's always possible to explain political events at multiple levels and to mix the 'tactical' with the contingent. By this time, Campbell Newman had provided a convenient scapegoat for all the LNP's woes, dumped on by his 'loyal' deputy Jeff Seeney just before the LNP ramped up its 'stay in government' noise machine. The Premier, after a few plaintive statements that he would still be there to save the day were a natural disaster to strike (although he has been conspicuous by his absence from actual floods and cyclone damage occurring in the north of the state), was reduced to cancelling and rescheduling LNP meetings by tweet, presumably sent from his perch high up in the Executive Building on George Street.

Newman then, still had his uses, precisely as scapegoat. That's not to say that his combative personality and his thin skin did not play a role in the unprecedented turn of the electoral pendulum in Queensland. As I've argued, clearly it did. Nevertheless, had the LNP chosen a more orthodox route to power in 2012, and I'm one who couldn't understand why they believed that John-Paul Langbroek would lead them to defeat against an unpopular fifth-term government, and thus had to install Newman as leader, odds are that the ALP would still have been defeated very badly indeed. Anna Bligh might have magnified the scale of that defeat by her relentless insistence that Newman and his family were allegedly entangled in the mire of dodgy deals and donations, and indeed her inability to prove her allegations was a turning point that prefigured the near wipeout of her party. But the combination of the accumulation of years of scandals and grievances and the breach of faith with voters on privatisation would still have been more than enough to send Labor packing.

That Queensland's voters sent Campbell Newman packing, returning Labor with a larger two-party preferred majority of votes than Anna Bligh enjoyed in 2009, despite its minority share of parliamentary seats, suggests that there is no turning back the clock. Queenslanders were open to a change of government, and happy for a new administration to sweep the broom clean after a series of scandals and a perception of declining public service standards. It also shows, however, that they were not happy for Joh's ghost to stalk the land again, and wanted a society and a polity characterised by openness, transparency and accountability. If even KAP state leader Rob Katter can laud these values at a conference just after the election, then the modernisation project has a momentum that may endure.

THIS IS QUEENSLAND, ANYTHING CAN HAPPEN

Jason Wilson, whom we met tweeting that seismic political events originate in Queensland, astutely points us in the direction where we should be looking for structural explanations of #qldvotes. The Queensland State Election of 2015, which elevated Annastacia Palaszczuk to the premiership, is the culmination of a longstanding public distaste for both privatisation and lies – the two seemingly inevitably intertwined – and it's a rejection of austerity commensurate with what we're seeing in Europe. Another claim that is sometimes made, on the left this time, is that neoliberalism does not exist, and that there is nothing akin to austerity economics in Australia. Perhaps those who hold to this view might wish to come and live in Queensland.

QUEENSLAND

Probably much more significant than Campbell Newman's quirks of personality in explaining the result of the 2015 state election was the mass sackings of public servants, which wracked an economy already shaky from the GFC and the 2011 Queensland floods. Perhaps a state where the state so blatantly withdraws from any attempt to support its citizens through adversity, and one where the rhetoric of the small state is embraced so heartily as in the Peter Costello report, demonstrates that although austerity has been blocked in the Senate federally to a large degree, which is not to minimise the real consequences of the Abbott regime for many, it's been well and truly at work in Queensland as a basis for policy and not just talk.

Are Queensland voters different from those in the rest of Australia, then? Probably not, because Australians expect things from their governments – things like a social security net, infrastructure, sound management of the economy, respect for freedoms but concern for fairness and social justice, and high-quality education and health services to give everyone a shot at living the way they would like to. Both Campbell Newman's spectacular downfall and Tony Abbott's woes suggest that these values are not ephemeral but fundamental, and that voters will punish politicians who claim to uphold them but lie about that, and who embark on the dismantling of the state and the public sphere while indulging themselves in ideological fantasies and retributive wars on their opponents, real or imaginary. Newman governed as Abbott would have liked to had he not been blocked in the Senate.

What is interesting is that the Australian electorate is becoming more like the Queensland electorate has long been – relatively unattached to party and ideology, and prepared to embrace alternatives where they present themselves. Just as Clive Palmer and a host of others captured significant, and in the end decisive for the Senate balance of power, support in various and sundry states and territories, so too have Queenslanders voted for a real alternative to business-as-usual politics captive of big business and all its tricks and seductions – whether audit commissions or the repetition of idiotic mantras ('stable strong team with a strong plan') beloved of so-called strategists. The space that Labor has moved into in Queensland is not traditional Labor space, but that was always a different place in Queensland anyway – not reinforced by manufacturing redoubts but much more free-floating and as much rural as urban.

The highest swings in the state election, 20 per cent and above in seats on the outskirts of Brisbane to the north and south, are in electorates full of people in part-time, casual or insecure jobs in less-skilled occupations and vocations. These voters don't want a culture war against institutions, they want jobs, basic services from government and a better future for their kids. Thus Labor can appeal to them simultaneously with a focus on trades, skills and employment and a vision of a transition to a competitive future not reliant on mining alone, however much the detail needs to be filled in. A comment by one voter on social media – 'people in my street don't own coalmines or shares, we just want to work and to have our voices heard' – says it all. Hence Palaszczuk's repeated insistence on the 'dignity of work' and 'our assets'. The 'reform' three-card trick has been played out, and an awful lot of Queenslanders are no longer ready to believe assurances that reform that is good for mining companies or merchant bankers is good for them. Why? Because it's untrue – it's a lie.

Propagandist dinosaurs, such as notorious *Courier-Mail* columnist Des Houghton, may claim that Palaszczuk's victory and the factional makeup of her cabinet ('union bosses', 'socialist left'!) might portend a shift to socialism, but that is simply absurd, and as disconnected from reality as much of the nonsense that passes for political commentary or partisan advocacy in so-called news channels in this country. Rather, Labor has promised a much more consultative style of government, one much more attuned to finding a consensus than dividing and conquering. Whether or not that can be delivered will be as important to the ALP's chances of retaining government as the slings and arrows of outrageous economic fortune.

The swing to the ALP came not just from the LNP but also through a higher rate of Greens preferences and the decline of the KAP vote. Although she ran Ian Rickuss close in Lockyer, Pauline Hanson's day is done. Even Bob

THIS IS QUEENSLAND, ANYTHING CAN HAPPEN

Katter found out, probably to his own shock, that many of his own candidates wouldn't cop the homophobic and racist ads produced for him in 2012 by KAP apparatchik Luke Shaw, better known as the foreperson of 'Joh's jury'. Clive Palmer has run out of puff, but the fact that he stands for a more humane approach to refugees and eschews moral crusades is significant.

The Peter Wellingtons in Queensland, the Tony Windsors and Rob Oakeshotts in New South Wales and the Cathy McGowans in Victoria are harbingers of the future – people of integrity not wedded to ideology, concerned about probity and accountable to communities. Wellington supported Labor in 1998, and Peter Beattie won a smashing victory at the next election in 2001. The Greens are knocking at the door in the Sunshine State, too, competitive in Mount Coot-tha and running ahead of Labor in Noosa, and at long last they have an elected state spokesperson in Senator Larissa Waters. Greens preferences delivered Labor the government just as much as Peter Wellington did, and the days of bipartisan subservience to the mining industry need to end, or that support will not endure. Queensland can go in one of two directions electorally: back to a long-term pattern of stable Labor rule, or off in search of something different.

Something interesting happened to Labor in Queensland when it was smashed almost to smithereens on 24 March 2012. Reduced to a tiny caucus, power shifted from the Parliamentary Labor Party to unions and activist movements, and the ALP leadership capitalised on this electorally through embracing community campaigning. That's important because, although we are hardly seeing either a mass movement or a left utopia, we have seen a reorientation of power in Queensland back to the people. Whether that will endure is another question, and although Palaszczuk is right in saying that she's fought a 'David and Goliath' battle, and that the party has 'climbed Mount Everest', there's always another mountain on the horizon and the slingshot needs a keen aim as well as a sure hand. And as Queensland goes, so will Australia. Nothing can be taken for granted, and the political class needs to begin to listen to the people again.

STRANGE, BEYOND PRECEDENTS IN HISTORY

The early parliamentarians, apart from Robert Herbert, grandson of the Earl of Carnarvon, who arrived as (inaugural Governor) Bowen's private secretary and was subsequently elected as first premier, had little or no political experience. And Herbert too was a comparative novice. They were all represented as 'woefully barren of statesmanship', and generally lacking in 'knowledge and ability'. A civil servant, who arrived in 1862, found the small governing class imbued with 'great ignorance' and 'strange ideas' that 'would astonish those who think and read'. Apart from a rough and vacillating town versus country interest in their ranks, there was no initial sense of party formation or much hint of political principle among them. Politicians crossed the floor with ease, engaged in prolonged and acrimonious personal disputes and usually put opportunism first. Parliamentary procedures were little understood. Instead, due to the absence of any structures of local government, colonial politicians tended to behave as individual benefactors, lavishing promises of public works upon their numerically small constituencies in order to obtain election. This had resulted, lamented Bowen, in 'a confused and bustling scuffle of local agency', 'log-rolling' at the polls, a strong tendency towards regionalism in decision-making, and general extravagance. It was 'as if the fate of an English Ministry was to depend on the construction of public works in Tipperary or Donegal', he quipped.

Raymond Evans, *A History of Queensland*, 2007

A hundred and ten years after the foundation of the colony, political scientist Peter Boyce lamented that parliament rarely sat and, when it did, its proceedings were disorderly and rarely edifying, characterised more by abuse and personal vendetta than a calm process of legislative deliberation. In 2015, Campbell Newman's Waterloo Weekend was characterised by threats that seats that did not return an LNP vote would not benefit from the bonanza of boondoggles to be funded by asset sales, as well as his ranting about bikies and robotic repetition of his 'strong team' mantras. Ashgrove turned down its $118 million 'Strong Plan', and so did 35 other seats that changed hands from ALP to LNP. Joh had done something similar all the way back in 1977, warning voters in Mount Isa, on one of his endless peregrinations around his Sovereign State in the government jet, that if they were foolish enough to elect an opposition member, nothing good would come to them. Joh got away with this, but Campbell Newman's log rolling planked.

Instead of an administration caught somewhere between the reactionary and the resources-driven modernism of coalmines, coal seam gas and development at all costs (even if the state government has to subsidise uneconomic mines, and even if the Great Barrier Reef suffers), we now have a new ALP Government with women in the top two leadership roles, only the second time this has happened in Australia – Kristina Keneally and Carmel Tebbutt in New South Wales were the first all-female Premier and Deputy Premier team. Annastacia Palaszczuk and Jackie Trad, though, are the first two women elected from opposition to power. The Palaszczuk Cabinet, in a first for Australia, has a majority of women ministers – eight out of fourteen.

When I was an undergraduate Arts student at the University of Queensland, in my third year in 1988, Stacia Palaszczuk and I were both members of the campus ALP

Club and became friends. In student politics back then, not so long ago, the University of Queensland Union, founded in 1911, had had precisely two female presidents – Fleur Kingham (now a judge) in 1983 and Jillann Farmer in 1986. I was elected treasurer of the union in 1987, on a ticket dominated by Young Labor students and with only one woman, aside from the candidate for Women's Rights vice-president, running for the executive. Gender politics was polarised in the late 1980s – the Women's Rights collective existed in some degree of tension with the formal union structures, and when Annastacia was elected to fill a casual vacancy as Women's Rights Vice-President, her greatest achievement was to diminish this tension and to proceed from a place of conciliation rather than confrontation. She has begun her premiership in the same spirit.

Anna Bligh still faced misogyny from within the Labor Party – and it's significant that, writing in 1987, Peter Charlton obviously signalled 'radical feminists' as being beyond the pale in the ALP – and was subject as well to the vicious rumour mill that plagues the small circles of Brisbane gossip. Social change can happen very quickly, very quickly indeed, and there is little sense now that Palaszczuk's leadership and her female majority cabinet is something out of the ordinary, even if it is an obvious cause for celebration for many.

Similarly, in a state that was more hostile to immigration for longer than others, and also the object of much less immigration than even smaller states like South Australia because of its lack of manufacturing jobs, the granddaughter of Polish immigrant Leo Palaszczuk, who suffered in a Nazi labour camp during World War Two, can represent an astonishingly ethnically diverse electorate of Inala, piling up a first preference vote of 75.1 per cent, and leading a state that is far more cosmopolitan than it was even at the turn of the century. With the elevation of Murri MP Leanne Enoch to cabinet, there is also hope that some of the great injustices of the past against the state's Indigenous people – for example, the Stolen Wages scandal – may be righted. We can only hope.

NOW MIGHT BE A GOOD TIME TO START

If we return to where we began, to Rosie Scott's Queensland, which is a 'rich seedbed for the original, the flamboyant, the decadent, the extreme', we need to ask, once again, whether Queensland is becoming less different from the rest of Australia. I would argue that the rest of Australia is becoming more like Newmanland, characterised by wild electoral shifts, tragicomedies of governmental instability and political obsession played out in full public view, and a public longing for something better, for something more honest, for a politics that privileges the public and treats citizens with respect instead of arrogant disdain. The media might still be the 'chooks to be fed' that they were in Joh's mind, but the electors have grown up. There are multitudes

THIS IS QUEENSLAND, ANYTHING CAN HAPPEN

of explanations for Queensland's difference, not quite as many as there are Queenslanders, but a plethora nevertheless. You can pick and choose, like the Rousseauist view that the tropical climate lends itself to corruption and lassitude, that it's so hot and stinky that it's easier to put your feet up and have a beer rather than protest or take responsibility for the governance of the state.

I write these words in the QUT Library at Gardens Point, a stone's throw from Parliament House and right next to the old Government House where Sir George Ferguson Bowen no doubt put his feet up and lamented the quality of the local crop of colonial politicians. A tropical cyclone is about to hit Rockhampton, and I can look out the window and see palm trees swept in the rain and the wind framed against QUT's utilitarian architecture. Walking past Parliament House to get here, my mind turned to the comment Peter Simpson of the Electrical Trades Union made a couple of days ago when union leaders met the new premier: 'The first time I can walk through the House without being shadowed by two or three cops'. The shadow of the police state has evaporated, and there's a new vibe – something more akin to the modern and democratic polity so many have strived for over such a long period of time. Queensland will always be different; it will always have its magical qualities, but there is no reason, none at all, why its citizens can't live their lives and dream their dreams confident that the state will be a servant not an oppressor, and that their rights, individually and collectively, will be secured for them.

Far from the apathy that is often said to characterise modern Australian politics, what we've just seen in Queensland over the past three years is an end to complacency and a determination to take back democratic rights that belong to the people. I hope we have seen the last of a tendency to slip back into a darker past, and I am confident that having lived temporarily in Newmanland, we now know that it's up to all of us, not just our elected leaders, to smooth over the potholes along the road to ever renewed modernity.

NOTES ON SOURCES

Much of the content of this book comes from my own stock of knowledge and reflection on Queensland culture and politics, having lived 45 of my 47 years in the state. Specific sources that were useful in researching the book include the following.

GENERAL HISTORIES

Raymond Evans (2007), *A History of Queensland*, Cambridge University Press, Melbourne/New York.

Ross Fitzgerald (1984), *From 1915 to the Early 1980s: A history of Queensland*, University of Queensland Press, Brisbane.

Ross Fitzgerald (2009), *Made in Queensland: A new history*, University of Queensland Press, Brisbane.

POLITICAL BIOGRAPHIES

Peter Beattie with Angelo Loukakis (2005), *Making a Difference: Reflections on life, leadership and politics*, HarperCollins, Sydney.

Ross Fitzgerald (1994), *'Red Ted': A biography of E.G. Theodore*, University of Queensland Press, Brisbane.

Paul Reynolds (2002), *Lock, Stock & Barrel: A political biography of Mike Ahern*, University of Queensland Press, Brisbane.

Rae Wear (2002), *Johannes Bjelke-Petersen: The Lord's premier*, University of Queensland Press, Brisbane.

QUEENSLAND POLITICS

Peter Charlton (1987), *State of Mind: Why Queensland is different*, Methuen Haynes, Sydney.

Matthew Condon (2010), *Brisbane*, NewSouth, Sydney.

Ross Fitzgerald & Harold Thornton (1989), *Labor in Queensland: 1880 to 1988*, University of Queensland Press, Brisbane.

Alan Metcalfe (1984), *In their Own Right: The rise to power of Joh's Nationals*, University of Queensland Press, Brisbane.

Denis Murphy, Roger Joyce, Margaret Cribb & Rae Wear (eds) (1990), *The Premiers of Queensland*, University of Queensland Press, Brisbane.

Julianne Schultz (ed) (2008), *Griffith Review: Hidden Queensland*, no. 21, ABC Books, Sydney.

Bron Stevens & John Wanna (eds) (1993), *The Goss Government: Promise and performance of Labor in Queensland*, Macmillan, Melbourne.

Geoffrey Stokes, Michael Leach & Ian Ward (eds) (2000), *The Rise and Fall of One Nation*, University of Queensland Press, Brisbane.

John Wanna & Tracey Arklay (2010) *The Ayes Have It: The history of the Queensland Parliament 1957–89*, ANU E Press, Canberra.

ACKNOWLEDGMENTS

First and foremost, I am exceptionally grateful to Phillipa McGuinness and Emma Driver at NewSouth for commissioning and believing in this work, and for all their help at all stages of the writing and editing process. Joanne Holliman did a superb job as an editor, too, and I am very grateful to her. Thanks also to Fiona Sim for skilful proofreading, to Michael Fox for helping me proofread and to Trevor Matthews for compiling the index.

One of the central insights that informed my thinking about Queensland political culture and history I owe to Associate Professor Michael Leach of Swinburne University, a friend of mine since my undergraduate days in the Department of Government at the University of Queensland.

For stimulating conversations about Queensland politics, mostly on Facebook, I am grateful to Sacha Blumen, Megan Inglis, Antonio Ferreira-Jardim, Michael Leach, Andrew Stafford, Martin Bush and other commenters on threads about #qldvotes. On Twitter, it was great to interact with observers of Queensland politics such as Margot Kingston and John Quiggin.

I've been writing online about Queensland politics

since 2006, initially for *Crikey*, where successive editors Misha Ketchell, Jonathan Green, Sophie Black and Jason Whittaker were consistently great to work with, particularly when elections came around. I'm proud to have been associated with *Crikey* in innovative forms of campaign coverage, including 'Pineapple Party Time' in 2009 and 'Behind the Seams' in 2012.

More recently, it was great to write about Queensland politics for *Guardian Australia* and *The Monthly*, and I thank Adam Brereton and Gabrielle Jackson at the *Guardian* and Bridget Maidment and Russell Marks at *The Monthly*. Thanks also to Jacinda Woodhead at *Overland* for publishing some reflections on the 2015 state election result, prompted by a Twitter discussion. Thanks to all these publications for allowing me to rework some material that originally appeared as campaign commentary.

Sara Synnot helped immensely in critiquing and encouraging me as the book proceeded, particularly with structure, and I'm immensely appreciative.

The State Library of Queensland and Brisbane City Council's Brisbane Square Library were great places to work, and are repositories of fabulous sources of information on Queensland.

The book was written in Chiang Mai and Surat Thani in Thailand, Singapore, Erskineville in Sydney, and Yandina, Ashgrove and Coolum in Queensland.

INDEX

Abbott, Tony 7, 131, 137, 141, 154–55
Ahern, Mike 65, 79, 80–82
Ahern government 80–83
ALP *see* Australian Labor Party
Anderson, Jessica 40
Ashgrove electorate 138, 140, 141
Atkinson, Sallyanne 11
austerity measures 108–9, 139–40, 153–54
Austin, Brian 66, 82
Australian Labor Party
   deals with Nationals and Liberals 65
   2015 election victory 132–33, 138–39, 145–46
   factionalism 94–96
   impact of 2012 defeat 106–8, 144, 157–58
   internal reform 94–96
   Queensland Split 57–58

Beattie, Peter 22, 79, 93–96, 97–98
Beattie government 91, 96–98, 107
Beddall, David 13
The Big Fellow (Palmer) 48
bikie laws 115
'Bjelkemander' *see* gerrymander
Bjelke-Petersen, Agneta 18
Bjelke-Petersen, Flo 66
Bjelke-Petersen, Joh
   downfall and trial 74, 75, 79
   elevation to ministry 63
   from 'Joe' to 'Joh' 64

'Joh for PM' 43, 78–79
   knighthood 70–71
Bjelke-Petersen, John 131–32
Bjelke-Petersen government 64, 68–78
Bleijie, Jarrod 116, 117
Bligh, Anna
   Queensland floods 19, 99–100
   stubbornness on privatisation 98, 99, 102, 151
Bligh government 98–102, 108
Bond, Alan 70
Borbidge, Rob 89, 91, 149
Borbidge/Sheldon government 89–90
Brisbane
   destruction of heritage 60–61
   distinctiveness 39–41, 48
   2011 floods 19, 99–100
   impact of postwar immigration 59
   lack of tourist icons 35–36
   lord mayors 135
   radical history 114–15
   underworld nightlife 76–77
by-elections
   Mundingburra 85, 89
   Redcliffe 118
   Stafford 118

Carmody, Tim 116–17
Casey, Ed 95
Chalk, Gordon 63, 65
Charlton, Peter 78

QUEENSLAND

Chief Justice appointment 21, 116–17
Commission of Audit report 108–10, 123, 154
Community Cabinets 91
Condon, Matt 39, 41
Confederate Action Party 11
consultative style of government 91
Coomera 10–12, 14
Cooper, Russell 82–83, 90
corruption *see* crime and corruption; Crime and Misconduct Commission; Criminal Justice Commission; Fitzgerald Inquiry
Costello, Peter 109–10, 123, 154
country humour 15–18
Country Party 64
crime and corruption 59–60, 71–72, 74–77, 80, 82, 84, 88–89, 96–97, 139
Crime and Misconduct Commission 119
Criminal Justice Commission 84, 90
Cunningham, Liz 89, 119

Davis, Arthur Hoey 13
Davis, Chris 118–19
Davis, Peter 117
Democratic Labor Party 58
Dempster, Quentin 72–73, 77
development at all costs 5, 42–43
Dick, Cameron 11
doctors, attack on 117–20
Drayton 50
Duhig, Archbishop James 81

Edwards, Lew 65
Elder, Jim 97
elections: federal
 1990: 13–14
 1993: 10–12, 14
elections: Queensland
 1974: 143–44
 1983: 32, 66, 144
 1986: 66, 72–73, 75
 1989: 83
 1996: 87
 1998: 91–92, 111
 2001: 22
 2009: 98
 2012: 104–8, 144, 151
 2015:
  campaign 127–38, 145–46
  LNP denies defeat 149–50
  result 139–43, 155–57
  significance and implications 141–43, 146–48, 151–52, 153–58
 landslide victories 7, 22, 64, 97, 106, 111, 143–44
 rise of splinter parties 111–12
 three-cornered contests 65
Electoral and Administrative Review Commission 84
electoral corruption 97
electoral malapportionment 51–52, 64, 73
electoral reform 51–52, 84
Electrical Trades Union 74
Enoch, Leanne 146, 162
environmental issues 28
ephemerality
 Brisbane 40, 48
 Gold Coast 41–43
Evans, Mike 66
Evans, Raymond 24, 27–28, 31, 34, 39, 114, 158–59

Ferrier, Carole 62, 114
Fitzgerald, Tony 21, 126, 139
Fitzgerald Inquiry 10, 74, 80, 84
floods (2010–11) 19, 99–101
fluoridation of drinking water 123
Forster, Robert 67
Four Corners broadcast 74
Fraser, Andrew 99
Fraser, John 120

INDEX

Gair, Vince 57–58
gambling *see* illegal gambling
gender issues 160–61
Georges, George 95
German immigrant farmers 12, 18
gerrymander 64, 73
Golconda (Palmer) 46–47
Gold Coast 41–43
Goldsworthy, Kerryn 39–41
Goss, Wayne 82, 85, 89
Goss government 51–52, 84–89
Greenmount 13, 15–16
Greens 157
Gunn, Bill 74

Hall, Rodney 40
Hanlon government 51
Hanson, Pauline 90–91, 132, 156
Hayden, Bill 95
Hinze, Russ 10, 75, 76, 79, 82

illegal gambling 75–77
Innes, Angus 65
irony and self-irony 17–18, 19

'Joh for PM' 43, 78–79
Jones, Alan 130, 136
Jones, Kate 138
judiciary, attack on 115–17

KAP (Katter's Australian Party) 105, 111, 132, 136, 148–49, 152, 156–57
Katter, Bob 6, 17, 93, 103–4, 106, 122, 156–57
Katter, Rob 152
knighthoods 70, 72
Knox, William 65

landslide election victories 7, 22, 64, 97, 106, 111, 143–44
Lane, Don 64, 66, 82
Lane, William 56

Langbroek, John-Paul 123, 147–48, 149
Last Drinks (McGahan) 48–49
Latour, Bruno 3–4
Laver, Brian 62
Lee, Gerard 2–3, 60
Lee Long, Rosa 92
Levy, Ken 119
Lewis, Terrence 75, 82
Liberal National Party (LNP) *see also* Newman government
   attempts 'constitutional coup' 149–50
   factionalism within 121
   leadership issues 134–36, 149
Liberal Party, conflict with Nationals 65
licensing laws 88
Life Rarely Tells (Lindsay) 47
Lindsay, Jack 47
LNP *see* Liberal National Party; Newman government
log-rolling 159
Lutheran Church 12, 18
Lynham, Anthony 118

Malouf, David 48
Masters, Chris 74
Maynard, Ian 120
McGahan, Andrew 9, 48–49
McMurdo, Margaret 117
modernity 3–5
Mundingburra by-election 85, 89
Murphy, Dennis 95

National Party
   captures seats in Brisbane 66
   common interests with Labor Party 14
   rivalry with Liberals 14
Newman, Campbell
   calls early election 128–29
   combative personality 113, 151
   loses own seat 141

as scapegoat 150–51
sues Jones for defamation 130, 136
Newman government
austerity programme 108–10
blitzkrieg character 110–11, 115–21, 122–23, 125–26, 127–28, 136, 144
disdain for evidence and consultation 110, 115, 123–24
2015 election campaign 128–39
2015 election defeat 139–43
2012 election victory 104–8, 113
lack of political experience 121
scorn for the public sector 119–20, 123–24, 126
'strong team' mantra 128, 137, 139, 142, 155
Nicholls, Tim 138
Nicklin, Frank 58–59
Nowra, Louis 103–4
Nuttall, Gordon 97

O'Neill, Dan 62
One Nation 91–93, 111, 132
'one vote one value' 51–52
organised crime 74
Orr, Graeme 150
Outlaw and Lawmaker (Praed) 49

Palaszczuk, Annastacia
background 160–61
elected Labor leader 144–45
2015 election campaign 132–33, 139
Minister for the Arts 2–3
Palaszczuk government 160–61
Palmer, Clive 21–22, 41, 43–46, 157
Palmer, Vance 46–48
Palmer United Party (PUP) 111–12, 131–32
Paterson, Banjo 37–38
'Pig City' (song) 68, 71–72
Pizzey, Jack 63

police corruption and misbehaviour 74–77, 82, 88–89
police repression 68, 70–71
police surveillance 69, 163
Police Union 90
populism 93–94, 111–12
Praed, Rosa 49
Pratt, Dorothy 91–92
Premier's Literary Awards 2, 110
Prince Philip knighthood 137
privatisation 96, 98–99, 102, 108, 198
Proctor, Roderick 72
property development 42–43
public servants, mass sackings 109, 110, 126, 154
PUP *see* Palmer United Party

Queensland Labor Party 57–58
Queensland's distinctiveness
bizarre politics 21
distance and diversity 50–56
end of? 162–63
government longevity 7
innate conservatism 114
kinship connections 12, 18
laconic country humour 15–18
rigours of climate 24
as unknowable 39, 46–48
writers' depictions and explanations 1–2, 24, 27–28, 31, 39, 158–59

radicalism 62, 114–15
rock music 60, 62, 66–67
Rudd, Kevin 85–86, 91, 93
Rudd, Steele 13
Rundle, Guy 41, 45–46

Schultz, Julianne 84, 86
Scott, Rosie 1–2
sectarianism 81
Seedtime (Palmer) 47
Seeney, Jeff 126, 131, 136, 150

INDEX

self-identity 19
SEQEB strike 74–75
Shaw, Luke 75, 157
Sheldon, Joan 90
Shepherdson Inquiry 97
sixties' counter-culture 60–62
Skase, Christopher 70
Sobronoff, Walter 117
Sparkes, Robert 66, 79
splinter parties of the right 111–12
Springbok Tour 64
Springborg, Lawrence 121, 134–35, 147–48, 149
Stafford, Andrew 127–28
Stafford by-election 118
states of emergency 64, 74
Stevens, Ray 42
student radicalism 62
Sunshine Coast 43–46
Swan, Wayne 83, 86

Tanti, Frank 89
'The Joke' 75–78, 88–89, 143

Theodore, 'Red' Ted 46
Thompson, Mitch 62
three-cornered contests 65
Toowoomba 53–54
Trad, Jackie 160
12 Edmondstone Street (Malouf) 48

University of Queensland 61–62, 98, 161

VLAD (Vicious Lawless Association Disbandment) laws 115

Warburton, Neville 73
'War on Doctors' 117–20
Waters, Larissa 157
Waterson, DB 50
Wellington, Peter 46, 91, 116, 143, 157
Wertheim, Peter 62
White, Terry 65
Woodforth, Jason 123

Printed and bound by CPI Group (UK) Ltd, Croydon, CR0 4YY
12/01/2026

14806250-0001